MW01275283

No Such Thing as a Bully

- Shred a Label, Save a Child

Bullyproofing Protection for Parents and Children

By Kelly Karius BSW
and Dr. Ron Graham DrE

Published by
Karius & Associates
www.kariusandassociates.com
Copyright 2011 to Kelly Karius

ISBN 978-0-9736831-3-4

Cover Design by Cynthia Mikolas, Photo by fotilia.com

These organizations know that our children create our communities. Please support the sponsors of The No Such Thing as a Bully® program and books for parents in your community!

4809 50th St
Consort AB
T0C 1B0
1-403-577-2360
1-888-577-2370

www.rogerejohnsonenterprises.ca

Appliances	Automobile Insurance
Home Entertainment	Property Insurance
Communication	Commercial Insurance
toddl@xplornet.ca	cindyl@xplornet.ca

Neutral Hills Learning & Community Connection Centre
403-577-3011

Under the direction of the Neutral Hills Community Adult Learning Society

3

FCSS Family and Community Support Services

Consort and Special Areas 4
403-577-3011

101 Palliser Trail
Box 670
Hanna, Alberta,
Canada
T0J 1P0
403-854-4481
800-601-3898
Consort School
403-577-3654

Note to parents:

This is a lifetime book. You can start using it as soon as you get it, but the most important thing you must understand is that there is no ending point for the use of the material. *It is lifetime material.*

In the best interests of your children, you will need to review this book from time to time. YOU, after all, are the major influence on your children, and when you learn and use these skills, and gain an understanding of the problem of bullying, you can teach your children.

Guidance happens daily. This material, while introduced lesson by lesson, will show up in everyday situations. YOU are the only one who can teach your child through every day situations. You are the one who will see the teachable moments. When you know the material well – and live it – you are going to be able to teach it very well. A little effort on your part will go a long way toward bully-proofing your children, and raising adults who will make a difference in the world. Bully-proofing doesn't just mean protecting your children from having bully actions used against them. It also means preventing your children from using bully actions, and raising children who are strong enough to stop bully actions when they see them.

As you discuss these issues with your child, watch your own reactions. If you react with strong emotions to what your child says, your child may shut down. Be sure to simply accept what your child is saying, then together you can plan strategies for managing any problems that come out. Use the modules to build your relationship, to understand your child's life. It will be time well spent.

Table of Contents

Introduction

The day you have your baby, you have more emotions than you ever thought you could have. You lovingly wrap, feed and change your precious bundle. As your child grows, you spend time wondering, worrying and childproofing. You protect. You'd give up your life to protect that precious child.

You don't want your child to be hurt by his own actions, any more than you want him to be hurt by someone else.

One day your precious little man, no longer quite so little, seems "off". You can't quite put your finger on it, but he's not quite his usual happy self. You ask what's wrong. "Nothing, I'm okay," he says. You stay a bit concerned.

Time moves on.

Another day, you see a bad bruise on his leg and hip. "We were playing dodgeball," he explains. "Boys", you might say, and ruffle his hair.

Time moves on.

Your son suddenly has a stomach ache that has lasted for two days. The trouble is unclear. You tell him that sometimes when people are upset, they actually get physical pain, and you ask him if anything is bothering him. He starts to cry.

It turns out that relationships have been created in the school that your son doesn't know how to handle. Bigger boys have been picking on him. He's trying to be a sport about it, laugh along or just avoid it, but they scare him. He's been pushed down, called names and had his homework taken from him. Lately he has felt afraid to go to school, but also afraid to tell anyone how he's feeling. Even his parents. He begs you not to go to the school.

Now what?

This familiar scene is played out in households across our nations. It involves boys and girls of all ages. It leaves parents and children scared and confused. School organizations feel helpless. Sometimes the bullying spreads to the internet and a child cannot avoid their tormentors even in their own home.

Each time this happens, another scene plays out in another home. A parent gets a call about a child who is using bully actions against another child – or hears a story about an argument and doesn't know how to handle it. Maybe a parent knows exactly where the bullying behavior is coming from, but doesn't have the resources or knowledge to put a stop to it.

This book is for both sets of parents. Sometimes you are angered by each other. You have different perspectives and you think you have different goals. But you don't. You aren't on different teams. Your children all need the same life skills to move them forward and teach them different and more positive ways of interacting with others.

You must have the tools to examine your own thinking and behavior and transfer those skills to your children. This version of **No Such Thing as a Bully**® will teach you how to work with your child to overcome bully actions.

Rationale and Goals

This book will not use the more common terms "bully" and "victim", replacing these labels with **bully actions** and **victim responses.** We believe every person has the capacity to use both types of behaviors in certain situations or with certain individuals. We believe that telling a child that he is a victim or a bully increases the chance the behavior will continue. It puts the child into a box. Once we see a child by a label, we may miss everything else that child can be. Talking about bullies and victims also minimizes the role of the bystander. Every child needs a skill set that will keep them mentally healthy.

We believe it is important for adult role models to check in with their own behavior and be aware of the responses they are modeling for the children around them. Habits can be changed. Childhood provides an abundance of teaching opportunities to help children make positive choices about how they will communicate, build their self concept and build their relationships with the people around them. We believe you can change actions and responses. Children who can overcome bullying are well-positioned to navigate conflict in their adult lives. It is our responsibility to teach them how.

Goals:

- To move parents from seeing their child as a bully or a victim to understanding that these are patterns of behavior that can be changed.
- To teach parents how to strengthen bystander children.
- To provide tools that assist with prevention and intervention in bullying situations.
- To teach parents tools that can change thinking patterns and increase self-confidence, and how to transfer that knowledge to their children.
- To help parents understand the dynamics and outcomes of bullying.
- To provide parents with ideas and tools to approach bullying situations.

Kelly's Story

Throughout my life, I have learned that I can make conscious changes to my own behavior. I have seen that the way I act and react affects the responses of those around me in every situation. I believe as a result that, person by person, bullying act by bullying act, bullying can be controlled.

The pendulum swung for me as I learned how to communicate properly and how to make things happen. I moved from experiencing bullying to being a bully, to fighting bullying.

In my home, "tough" was a value. I was a gentle soul and had trouble acclimating to that. My dad used to tell my mom he had trouble disciplining me because I cried too quickly. I definitely remember the phrase "Stop crying, or I'll give you something to cry about!" being thrown around. I remember a lot of horseplay between my two brothers, but I was treated differently. Well, except for that one time when I was a baby and they tried to put me in the dryer. The most traumatic physical things that I experienced were being spanked occasionally - mostly a quick backhand on my butt from my mom as I was going by - and being tickled until I almost peed. I wasn't competitive, either. I had trouble understanding why they only used one puck for hockey when there was a whole pail of pucks in the scorekeeper's box. Why were they all fighting about one silly puck when there was enough for everyone?

I was always the big kid in elementary school. I recall thinking that I was fat, but when I look back at pictures it's clear that I wasn't. Still, I was definitely taller and broader than all the other girls in the class. That's OK when you're a boy; not so much when you're a girl. I remember being weighed in class, and all our weights being written on the chalkboard. I was the first one to get past a hundred pounds in grade 5, making the sting of my hated nickname – Kelly jelly smelly belly – even worse. I remember social isolation from girls who, now, as women, probably feel terrible about some of their actions. I recall two of my friends and myself all wearing white on the same day in school. We were called clouds, and the others stopped talking to us for a few days. How very random is that? The three of us continue to be friends. But I've also reconnected with some of those other girls. Some who may even read this, and recognize themselves and be sad about their actions. I don't write this to make anyone sad. We were unregulated, bullying wasn't talked about – yet it still existed, with all the same symptoms we see now. The girls and boys who I felt bullied me are now women and men. I continue to know most of them, and I like them. They are not the same people they were, nor am I.

Looking back to Junior High makes me understand that through all of this, my self-concept was completely out-of-whack. I wasn't sure who I was, and the parts of me that I was sure about were negative to me. I was looking for my self concept in the comments of others.

In Junior High I started to buy into the idea of "tough" as a value. Tough made people scared of me. No one called me Kelly jelly smelly belly anymore. A new Kelly emerged: who always wore a jean jacket, smoked in the school bathroom and beat up a boy in the boy's bathroom when he was going to tell.

This Kelly played Juice Newton's *Playing with the Queen of Hearts* from her locker while *O Canada!* was on the school speakers, and lipped off to teachers. Junior High Kelly spent a bit of time in the Principal's office. My heart was still good. I wanted to help people. I knew there were things I was doing that were wrong, but I was the tough class clown and I wasn't willing to sacrifice that for Kelly jelly smelly belly. My new nickname was Orv – there were a few of us in the school that were honored with our opposite parent's name as a nickname. It meant you were accepted to some extent. I apologize to those I hurt in junior high school. You know who you are. And there may be some people that I've hurt without even knowing. I apologize for that too.

In high school, I found an even keel, becoming the girl that most people liked and hardly anyone teased. There was no longer need for the misplaced, ill-fitting, tough persona that I had carried. I learned the freedom of

13

helping others, the social connection of listening and being a good friend. I am honored to have many lifetime friendships with people from all parts of my school years.

For me, there was an innate sense of right and wrong, of empathy for others that kept me from heading too far into the bullying path. Underneath my journey to the path, and my sense of victimization in school was an inaccurate belief that I wasn't good enough. That somehow, you had to be a certain weight, and have a certain look in order to have value. That if you can't achieve those things naturally, then you act in ways that you perceive to give you value.

Training as a Social Worker, and later exposure to families and children who were struggling with bullying issues on an ongoing basis, solidified my desire to not only find that even keel, but to advocate for change. Big change.

The world needs to learn to work with its children, not just before school but through childhood and beyond, to remind them that we are who we are, and that we have value just because we are. Children must be told they are beautiful, inside and out. Differences must be noted, celebrated without becoming a focus. Social media myths must be addressed. Children must understand that they don't have to look like a supermodel or an avatar. We are who we are and we are blessed and valued. They must understand that over and over. We don't create their journey, but we do contribute. As an adult, you must understand these things about yourself as well – then you must transfer them to your children.

Ron's Story

I looked at a map of my hometown and started drawing on it. I drew three circles in orange to show the schools I attended. A fourth circle indicated my home. I started drawing X's on the map to show where I was bullied. There are nearly 40 of them...and might be more, but I can't put them on top of each other. At about half of those X-marks-the-spots, I was beat up. In one case, I was nearly put in the hospital by three boys. It's hard for me to point out specific incidents of bullying in my childhood to write about, because there are so many, they all simply run together into this big old mess. So I decided to write about the mess.

I have ADHD, which means I alternate between being distractible and being hyperfocused. Either way, it's complete. Over the years, I've learned coping skills, but in those days, children with this condition were something teachers didn't know what to do with. I was smart, heavens yes, but the behaviors associated with ADHD (then called "Minimal Brain Defunctness" if anyone called it anything at all), such as often being in motion and/or talking loudly, made me a target for teasing – and worse. I was a bullying magnet.

I've often referred to myself as a "mark." One "bully" could pick on me and get a response – usually crying or a complete meltdown – and others would see that as entertainment and arrange to get their share. A mark is ostracized from the school's "society."

Nobody would stick up for me. Nobody would testify on my behalf if I went to the Principal or to a teacher. A couple of times, I would receive the same whack with a paddle that those who picked on me got, and then I'd get it from them again later. Nowhere in the school was safe. The teachers never seemed to catch those who made my life miserable on that particular day. Home was safe – but I had to GET there. I walked to and from school every day until halfway through my senior year of high school.

What did I do? What COULD I do?" I wasn't going to kill myself, because you only have hope of a better tomorrow if you are alive to see it. So I did the following:

 - I grew a sense of humor.

 - I learned to keep opinions to myself except for what's relevant in class. Because if you were a mark, those who bullied you would use your opinions to target you.

 - I started to be serious about making friends, and staying as close to them as opportunity would allow.

 - I grew temporarily deaf when within hearing distance of those who wanted to target the mark.

Some people my age – including those from my hometown and school district – moan about the attention paid to bullying, and how they faced the same problems and grew up strong. That is an incorrect view of our growing-up years. I was terribly lonely and desperately afraid to take my next step. My experience tells me that the current rash of "bullycide" has been inevitable, and it's foolish to ignore the way the kids (especially the "marks") are treated because it'll somehow "make them grow up strong." That's nonsense – dangerous nonsense.

I try not to be bitter. Writing this, I was actually afraid of bringing up old wounds. Some of those who beat me up are now dead, after all, and I don't wish to be bitter. But childhood pain never really dies. So I treat it by trying to help others who may now be facing what I faced. I'm on a mission now, to save our sons and daughters – while we still can. And you better believe we still can.

Definitions

Term	Definition
Bullying	bully actor perspective + action + victim responder perspective (see below) Bullying may result in physical injury, hindrance of mental or emotional development and/or exploitation.
Bully Actor	A person who is engaging in a bullying action
Victim Responder	A person who is engaging in a victim response

Bullying can be described in equation form:[1]

Bullying = Bully Actor Perspective + Action + Victim Responder Perspective where	
Bully actor perspective =	desire to hurt + superior power/enjoyment + desire for control/contempt
Action =	hurtful + repeated
Victim Responder Perspective =	vulnerability + sense of oppression/unjust treatment

Definition adapted from Ken Rigby, and used with permission, http://www.kenrigby.net

Types of bullying include:
- *Physical*: striking another person; damaging or stealing another person's property
- *Verbal*: name-calling, teasing, humiliating or threatening
- *Social*: excluding others; spreading rumors; humiliation; interference in relationships
- *Cyber/Electronic*: verbal and/or social bullying via Internet or phone[2]
- *Sexual*: physical or verbal actions relating to one's sexual being or sexuality

The bully actor perspective contains the aspects of having a desire to hurt, and using harmful actions to create a sense of superiority and to control situations and people around them.

When the bully actor perspective is combined with hurtful and repeated action against someone who carries or may be prone to a victim response perspective, a bullying situation takes place. Someone who is prone to a victim responder perspective has a sense of vulnerability and helplessness. They feel incapable of protecting themselves from the bully and they portray responses that the bully responder finds entertaining, and which contribute to the illusion of the bully responder's sense of power and control.

We all have the capacity to bully others in particular situations and under certain conditions. But few of us will actually identify ourselves as bullies. For this reason, the phrases "bully actor" and "victim responder" are used here, rather than the words bully and victim. We don't wish to categorize anyone as either a full time bully or a full time victim. Rather, we wish to provide ways to assess which behaviors and attitudes constitute the bully action and the victim response, and eliminate these actions and attitudes. In this way, we work to eliminate bullying behavior, rather than eliminating or denigrating people.

The definition illustrates a fundamental power imbalance. It is when the power between people is unbalanced that bullying actions can escalate to a bullying situation.

Bystander behavior is a bully action when it supports the bully. Some bystanders feel the same emotions and intentions as the person using the bully actions. These are active supporters, and they are using bully actions as well. Some bystanders do not feel the contempt, control, desire to hurt and enjoyment that is required to define a bully action, but they may not stand up in defense of others because of fear, lack of self confidence, or lack of knowledge about what to do.

Ultimately, children using all three of the groups of behavior - bully actions, victim responses and bystander behaviors, need skills that help them positively build their self concept, balance their thinking, increase their self confidence, gain empathy and understanding, and learn superior communication skills.

Recognizing the signs

Children who are experiencing bullying actions against them might:

- be afraid of how they are getting to school.

- indicate they would like to make changes to their schedule.

- become afraid to go to school entirely.

- have mysterious and undiagnosed pains or illness.

- experience lower grades, and suffer in their school work.

- appear less confident.

- withdraw and/or become anxious.

- become aggressive with other children.

- have changes in appetite.

- not fully explain any bruises, cuts or scratches.

- have property go missing or be ruined.

- give excuses that don't make sense.

- act secretively and/or begin stealing.

- experience negative mood changes after interacting online or by cell phone.

Children who are using bully actions might:

- talk negatively and derogatorily about some of their peers.

- freely use negative labels contemptuously in conversation.

- portray themselves as a victim when their behavior is confronted.

- blame the other child.

- not see the need to apologize for their behavior.

- show contempt for other children.

- act differently in front of adults than in front of peers.

- have low levels of empathy.

- have extremely high or extremely low self-esteem.

- have previously experienced bully actions against themselves.

- have a role model who acts aggressively.

Children who are bystanders might:

- try to distance themselves from the actions.

- be fearful of the child using bully actions.

- try to stay friends with the child using bully actions.

- talk about conflict between their peers.

- try to figure out how to handle the situation without adult intervention.

- be afraid of the reaction of the child using bully actions if they stand up for another child.

- be open to strong leadership in the area of bullying prevention and intervention.

- be well placed to utilize bullyproofing tools in their schools and communities.

Approaching Your Child

If you see any of these symptoms, it is important for you to approach your child. Some ideas:

1. Try not to make a big deal of the approach, especially with older children. Make use of an activity together, or a time when you are driving with your child, to explore how his peer friendships and relationships are going. Be careful not to be judgmental.

2. Even if you are not concerned that your child is experiencing difficulties, discussing relationships is good practice. Starting to talk about peer relationships early sets the scene for talking about them in the later childhood years, when it tends to become more difficult.

3. If your child does not disclose any problem, but you are still concerned, focus on what you have seen. Tell your child about the changes you've noticed in him, or the things that you are seeing and ask about the cause. Give him details of what can be seen in the outer world. Ask directly if your child is experiencing or using bully actions, or being exposed to bullying at school. Assure your child that he can work with you on how to solve the problem.

4. Be careful not to create a problem where one did not exist before. A child may be experiencing bully actions, but if he is able to handle the situation on his own, with your coaching, he begins to gain his own life experience. Remember that conflict is a part of a child's life, just as it is a part of an adult's life. Conflict in childhood is the training ground for managing conflict well as an adult. It is important to understand the distinction between conflict and bullying and know when it is important to step in as a parent.

When a parent takes over for a child, rather than coaching children to handle their own small conflicts, opportunities for learning are missed. When conflict is minimized and a child is not coached along, learning opportunities are also missed. We must acknowledge the conflict in our children's lives and be aware of what they can handle on their own, and when they need adults to intervene. When a situation is bullying, and a parent intervenes, it must be done in a way that is proactive, positive and resolution focused.

5. If you are reacting strongly as a parent, self-examine your reaction. Were you bullied in school? Are you being bullied now? We tend to react strongly to situations that we connect with emotionally. It is not helpful to your child, in a bullying situation, for you to overreact. Plan your post-disclosure actions well, and clearly understand why you are taking your chosen steps.

6. Before approaching the school, do a risk assessment. Does your child feel he is in grave and immediate danger? If so, it is necessary to take action quickly. Don't be afraid to pull a child out of school until you figure out the situation, particularly in cases where situations have already become severe.

Risk assessment questions and other levels of intervention are provided next.

Risk Assessment

A risk assessment includes the following steps:
STEP 1: Evaluate the possibility of harm.
STEP 2: Evaluate current safety plans.
STEP 3: Evaluate effects.
STEP 4: Determine if there is a greater need for intervention.

1. What are the levels of bully actions that my child is experiencing? Rate each type of bullying (Physical, Verbal, Sexual, Cyber, Social) on a scale of one (not at all) to ten (very severe).

2. What processes are in place in the setting that provide safety for my child? Consider: School culture, school policy, child's friendships, adult support in the school

3. How is my child being affected? Using the list of effects in the "Recognizing the Signs" section, note the ones you are seeing in your child. Consider any other effects you are seeing as well.

   High numbers in question 1, low processes in question 2, and many effects in question 3, lets you know that you likely need to use several scales of intervention.

   A combination of medium numbers in question 1, consistent clear safety plans, and lower effects, lets you know that you need to provide intervention at the level of your child.

   This is not a scientific tool, but rather, is intended to provide a framework that encourages your ability to mindfully determine your next steps.

Levels of Intervention

Intervention with child:

Intervening directly with your child means teaching your child how to manage a bullying situation directly, through life skills, communication skills and tools that help to manage thinking and behavior.

Children using bully actions and victim responses both need the same skills. They may require different examples and different ways to understand the patterns of behavior, but the skills are the same.

In the second part of this book, you will learn the essential knowledge that is needed to manage both bully actions and victim responses. You will also learn how to transfer that knowledge to your children, regardless of how they are reacting.

Intervention with other parents/child:

Generally speaking, this is a step that needs to be taken very carefully. It is a good idea to lower your defenses prior to approaching the other parents. People will have a fight or flight reaction when they are approached if they are approached aggressively – and sometimes even if they are approached calmly. You must begin the conversation feeling that you are on the same team. Resolution involves moving from "me against you", to "us against the problem"[3] Another parent's response is going to be much more receptive if you are seeking solutions rather than approaching the situation with blame. If you are in the middle of a situation right now, and it feels that this type of perspective is an impossibility, then take the time to

---

[3] Dr. Daniel Dana, Conflict Resolution: Mediation Tools for Everyday Worklife, 2001

learn the skills in this book as you are making a final decision about your approach. Keep in mind that it is rare for an aggressive approach to have a positive outcome.

Decide ahead of time, what you wish to achieve by speaking with the other parent(s): Are you:

-trying to find out more information about the situation?
-Making them aware of their own child's behavior?
-Making them aware of your child's reaction?
-Hoping to come up with a collaborated solution?

If a primary reason for talking with the other child's parent is to voice your anger, or give them what you feel they 'deserve', reconsider. It is essential that your intention is to assist in resolving the issue peacefully, or your involvement can potentially increase the problems. Do not involve children in this process at the outset. Children should only be involved if they feel safe and if both sets of parents are working towards a collaborative resolution that involves apologizing for bully actions and moving forward in a way that is long term positive for the children involved.

It is possible that this intervention is more common for parents who find that their child is experiencing bully actions against them, however if you want to become truly proactive about managing bullying, then you must also examine your child's behavior in regard to how they are treating others.

If you say to yourself "my child would never hurt another child," have another look. There is a culture of hurt out there for children and it is difficult for all children to be able to stay out of it, even those that are seen as 'good' children. Keep your eyes open.

Intervention with schools:

Again, be sure that your approach is one that assures the school administration that you are on their side. They are not your enemy and if your approach treats them like the enemy, they will not respond as well as you are going to want them to – and you may harm future relationships with them.

Let the school know what you are doing at home to work on solving the problem. If the school feels that you are simply throwing it in their lap, they will not be as receptive to taking responsibility.

Be active in the school, get on the PTA committee, stay in touch with your child's teacher, and provide supervision at the school whenever you can. Get to know children that are using bully actions in a friendly, natural way. All adults are responsible for assisting with management in an environment where bully actions can take place. Remember that the child is not your enemy either. Both the children involved are exactly that, children.

For the child using either victim responses or bully actions, the intervention at the school level is the same.

Talk to your child's teacher about ways a particular child can be encouraged to become more assertive in school. Ask your school if they have, or are willing to arrange, a training program, such as *No Such Thing as a Bully®*, or other program for smaller groups of children in the school. Continue to be aware of your child's perception of safety if they have experienced bully actions. Believe your child if they tell you they are still afraid. Talk with the school counselor about your child's adaptation, and find out how the counselor is, or can help. Look for ways that you can be involved in the school in informal and supervisory capacities. Whether your child is using bully actions or victim responses, encourage your school to use the system of restitution (fixing the problem), resolution (figuring out a way to keep it from happening again), and reconciliation (finding ways to heal with the person one has harmed).[4]

Intervention with systems:

When you have approached the school and haven't received a response that is acceptable to you, you may choose to go a step higher and approach a school board or administration system.

Children are particularly at risk in schools that deny bullying problems, lack effective policies and procedures to address bullying, develop a culture of regimented cliques that are supported by administration and the culture in using bully actions, and have adults who avoid seeing and/or addressing bully actions.

If you decide to take this next step, do your research. You must approach the situation with an awareness of the policies and procedures involved in the organization's approach to bullying. Ask for a copy of the school and/or school division bullying policy. Look for others who have already done your research. There may be a group of concerned parents that you can join with, rather than taking a system change battle on your own. Think about who your support people are, and how they can help. Remember that the system generally holds more power than a disgruntled parent, and if your approach is too aggressive, it may be ignored or minimized. Approach the

---

[4] Barbara Coloroso, The Bully, The Bullied and the Bystander, 2004.

people who have a stake in the system with feasible solutions rather than simply throwing your problem at them.

We suggest you explore the option of a *No Such Thing as a Bully*® Community Immersion in your community. This will provide a change to the fundamental systems that are creating a problem. More information is found at http://nosuchthingasabully.com .

When a parent/teacher/adult is using bully actions

This is one of the most difficult situations. It must be approached with a great deal of assertive behavior. The adult must be approached in a way that helps him or her to understand the child's perceptions. It is likely that the adult is not going to immediately say, "Oh, hey, yeah, I AM a bully!", but they may be able to say "Okay, I can see how that may have come across wrong."

Adults often engage in bully actions. This work is intended to change their skill level in terms of assertive approaches and give them skills they didn't have, or help them more fully understand the skills they already do have. Children benefit the most when the adults that are teaching them understand how to live with flexible but clear, assertive boundaries. School policies and staff must also reflect assertive and thoughtful principles and actions.

If you suspect your child is being bullied by an adult, it is important to gather information from your child, about what they perceive is happening. When your child gets older, this gets easier. Present the information to the adult as the child's perception, and ask the adult to explain the situation, from their point of view. You may not receive satisfactory answers immediately, but it is important to then watch the follow up behavior. Sometimes simply challenging a behavior is enough to remove it.

If this is ineffective, and the adult is a teacher, you may have to extend involvement to the principal. If this is the route you decide to take, be sure your information is solid and well documented. You may choose to check options for changing primary classrooms, or, if the situation remains unresolved, you may even consider changing schools.

People in authority using their power in a bullying manner only happens occasionally, but when it does, you must be prepared to consciously evaluate the situation, not fly off the handle, and take steps to improve your child's situation, providing protection if necessary.

"Screen Time" and Bullying

While the research linking aggressive behavior in children to violent games and videos is not conclusive, as parents, we know that children are affected by the games they play.

Take a moment right now to think about the childhood games that YOU played. I bet you can name them, and attach memories to them. You know who you were playing them with, and you know how they made you feel.

Now picture the 11 year old in his room playing "Call of Duty", (all his friends have it, and mom didn't really LOOK at the game, he really wanted it.) He hears and throws out curses, he shoots people, he plays by himself with someone he met online, named Lintmuffin. Sometimes he plays with his friends. He immerses himself in war.

He moves from playing COD with Lintmuffin and his friends, to checking out his Facebook, takes a few pictures of himself, checks out a cruel fake page a couple of girls made about another girl, leaves a nasty comment.

31

Hopefully in there somewhere, he is also playing a healthy game of football, or spending time with his mom and dad, but he may not be. It is up to you to screen your child's games and make sure they are appropriate, as well as to limit the amount of time spent in this way. Life is all about balance.

Some things to watch for include:

- A child trying to deny your access to their computer or gaming systems.
- A child whose mood changes after being on the computer or checking their cell phone.
- A child who does not want their parents involved in any of the social media sites they use.

The more unsupervised and unquestioned time a child spends in front of an interactive screen, the more susceptible he become to cyber bully actions and victim responses. Monitor your child's use of the computer, cell phone* and games systems carefully and educate yourself about the danger.

*No Such Thing as a Bully is working with aBeanstalk to promote a safety application for your child. The app connects you with your child's social media pages and cell phone, sending you alerts as you choose, to help keep your child safe. Check out the free version at http://abeanstalk.com

Recognizing Bully Actions and Victim Responses

Bully Actor	Victim Responder
• Actions are impulsive and aggressive • Difficulty in regulating mood and high frustration levels • Actions may involve breaking the law • Remorse does not follow actions, lack of empathy • May be supported in their actions by peers and even by family. • Directs blame at others rather than at self • Underdeveloped relational problem solving skills • May be a response to authoritarian or inconsistent parenting • May be unskilled in evaluating their own behavior	• Actions are anxious, insecure or shy • May present as cautious, lacking confidence, passive • Few peer friends and supporters • May present as different from others in some way • Offers "entertaining" reactions • Directs blame at self • May feel discouraged about making any change in their situation. • May be afraid to ask for adult help, fearing that "tattling" will make the situation worse. • May be too embarrassed and/or humiliated to ask for help.

Bully Actors need to:	Victim Responders need to:
• learn limits • understand and accept responsibility for actions and consequences • control the "fight or flight" response • develop problem-solving skills • express emotions and communicate positively • be reinforced for expressing emotions positively • learn understanding and empathy • be given an opportunity to appropriately resolve the issue	• find social support in a safe setting • learn and grow in a safe setting • take pride in differences • develop assertive skills, including speech, attitude and body language • receive direct coaching in replying to bully actions • be safely involved in the consequences of bullying

Keep in mind that those using the bully action or the victim response defy stereotypes.

The descriptions of bully actions and victim responses don't change appreciably, whatever form the bullying may take:

- *Physical*: striking another person; damaging or stealing another person's property

- *Verbal*: name-calling, teasing, humiliating or threatening
- *Social*: excluding others; spreading rumors; humiliation; interference in relationships
- *Cyber/Electronic*: verbal and/or social bullying via Internet or phone[5]
- *Sexual*: physical or verbal actions relating to one's sexual being or sexuality

Bystanders play an extremely important role. It has been shown that the quickest way for bullying to stop is for bystanders to step up in defense of the child who is experiencing bully actions.

Every child is affected by bullying, if not directly, then as a bystander. Every child needs to be taught to identify and confront bully actions. They need to understand and appreciate differences, and understand the tragic potential effects of bullying.

Even if a child is not using or experiencing bully actions, approach them with this information from a bystander point of view. The bystander role is the most important one in this syndrome, and our youth must be strong enough and educated enough to be strong bystanders.

Children Experiencing Bully Actions

Symptom	Reason
Lack of interest in school or refusal to go to school.	Fear – logic – avoidance of bully actions.
Taking an unusual route to school.	Fear – Logic – avoidance of bully actions.
Experiences a negative mood change after receiving a phone call or email.	Sense of shame in talking about ugly calls.
Drop in grades	Lowered concentration, focus is on avoiding the bully action, or sometimes plotting revenge.
Withdrawal from family activities	Carrying a sense of humiliation and shame, fear of disclosure.
Withdrawal from peer activities	Humiliation and shame, fear of being in unprotected regions
Extreme after school hunger	Symptomatic of lunch or lunch money extortion
Stealing or asking for money more than usual	Symptomatic of extortion
Using the bathroom immediately at home	May indicate the bathroom at school is an unsafe place.

Predicting Violent Behavior

It is difficult to predict violent human behavior. We are an unpredictable species. Many can go through extremely traumatic ongoing incidences of violence and bullying and overcome them, while still living with the results. Other children may deal with what adults perceive as only a slight amount of violence and/or bullying before turning to violent behavior themselves. How the adults around them react and encourage them to react to the bullying issues they experience matters as well.

Indicators of escalated teen violence are listed by Becker[6]. These indicators include:

- Alcohol and drug abuse

- Addiction to media products

- Aimlessness (constantly changing goals and ambitions, unrealistic expectations, and lack of perseverance and self discipline to reach the goals).

- Fascination with weapons

- Experience with guns

- Access to guns

- Sullen, angry; depressed

- Seeking status and worth through violence

- Threats (of violence or suicide)

---

[6] Gavin de Becker, Protecting the Gift: Keeping Children and Teenagers Safe (And Parents Sane), 1999

- Chronic anger

- Rejection/humiliation

- Media Provocation: Widely-publicized major acts of violence can stimulate people who identify with the perpetrators and the attention they receive.

Daniel Goleman describes 7 key abilities people must have to effectively manage life[7]. These include:

- To motivate ourselves

- To persist against frustration

- To delay gratification

- To regulate moods

- To hope

- To empathize

- To control impulses

Essentially, many of these basic skills are untaught, except by example. And when a child is experiencing bully actions against him, it becomes difficult to manage the situation, if he has not developed these basic skills. These are the skills that keep our children ALIVE and WELL! The child without motivation cannot develop the energy to see the future, never mind to create it. The child that can not persist against frustration is not able to learn difficult concepts, or change negative behaviors. The child who can

---

[7] Daniel Goleman, Emotional Intelligence: Why it Can Matter More Than IQ, 1996

not delay gratification can not see tomorrow clearly. The child who cannot regulate his moods is unable to attach thought to emotion, and logically examine and change moods and circumstances.

The child who is unable to hope, becomes depressed, and often suicidal. The child who is unable to empathize turns to the same violence and anger that they are experiencing, at times taking great satisfaction and power in creating a new, angry, violent energy around themselves. Children unable to control their impulses have not learned to use forward thinking patterns to assess life.

This book actively teaches those skills to adults, and then teaches adults how to actively teach the skills to their children.

Bullying Outcomes

We know, many of us from personal experience, that the child bullied in school is not likely to feel safe, by night or day. If a child is beat up and/or terrorized, the child will spend the rest of the school year walking home along a different route, sometimes several different routes, in an attempt to avoid another beating or humiliation. Many children have spent entire school years adding many miles to their route home to avoid a confrontation. Many children have felt they must spend recess time in the close vicinity of a teacher. Many children have had trouble making friends, because other children, potential friends, don't want to risk becoming a target of bullying actions themselves. Those who define themselves, or who are defined as a victim, feel that THEY are unable to change or adjust their situation. They feel they must wait for some external change, a change in schools because of passing a grade, or some other outside force, such as the direct intervention of an adult.

And the consequences of bully actions/victim response can be even worse. Consider these after-effects to which those bullied by classmates can be exposed:

- Decline in quality of school work

- Problems with attendance

- Difficulty sleeping at night, perhaps nightmares, leading to school days exhausted and lethargic

- Avoidance of certain areas of the school, especially bathrooms, showers, gym – places where adults are frequently absent.

All this amounts not only to decreased performance in school, but also the loss of opportunity to make good friends and lasting hobbies. The long term effects of this can be loss of educational and/or employment opportunities. The loss of self esteem and loss of opportunity can lead those experiencing a victim response to themselves become violent offenders, and sometimes even to attempt or complete suicide or revenge.

The Bully Actor/Victim Responder Spiral

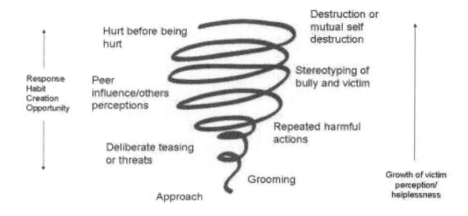

The Spiral indicates the cycle that is built when bullying actions are not addressed in a straight forward manner.

One person is approached by another person. If one person has learned to control by power, the grooming pattern includes testing; How will this person react to me? The teasing, threats and/or harmful actions continue and accelerate as long as the situation is not addressed and the victim responses are continuing. Bystanders play an important role in determining if the situation will continue to escalate or will be derailed. The players are likely to be characterized as a bully and a victim. The person using victim responses comes to see themselves as helpless. The person using bully actions learns that power works to get your own way. The 'victim' may, at some point, lash out with a bully action and may then be characterized as a bully instead of a victim. Ultimately, destruction to both parties may be experienced.

Real Life School Bullying

Dawn Marie Wesley

By November 10, 2000, Dawn-Marie Wesley, 14, of Mission BC had been dealing with bullying actions from several girls for many months. There had been a breakdown of friendships in her peer group, the result being several girls using bullying actions against Dawn-Marie. Rumors were spread about Dawn-Marie. Threats were made. Dawn-Marie felt it was necessary to speak to her school counselor daily and she was always sure not to walk home from school by herself. On this evening, one of the girls yelled at her over the phone "You are fucking dead."

Bystanders were co-opted into the group and assisted in the harassment or were silent about it. Only two of Dawn-Marie's friends tried to intervene.

Dawn-Marie was depressed and tired and scared. She must have felt she had nowhere to turn. She believed the girls were going to kill her or hurt her, writing in her suicide note that she had been threatened by bullies and believed death was her only escape. She said she was depressed and couldn't tell anyone about the abuse because the girls tormenting her would get suspended and then the situation would only get worse. One girl, who witnessed one of the girls threatening to kill Dawn-Marie, said: "I would have stopped it if I could, but it happened so fast."

She hung herself in her bedroom with her dog's leash, and was later found by her 13-year-old brother. Two girls were charged for uttering threats. One of the girls was additionally charged with criminal harassment. The girl that had been charged singly was acquitted. The girl with two charges was convicted. The offenders cannot be named because of the Young Offenders Act.

The defense argued that the bullying actions were normal schoolyard behavior and stated the teens never intended or planned to kill Dawn-Marie. The prosecution conceded that there may not have been intent to kill, however the accused terrorized Dawn-Marie, and that in itself is criminal behavior. This was an issue of bullying, the first of its kind to be tried in Canada.

According to B.C. Provincial Court Judge Madam Justice Jill Rounthwait, the question was narrow and legal. "When do school yard taunts cross over the line to become a criminal offence of threatening death or bodily harm? When does a teenager's annoying behavior towards a fellow student amount to an offence of criminal harassment?" These are the questions to which she applied the law.

Madam Justice Rounthwait said that it was clear that one of the accused had bullied Wesley repeatedly, giving the victim reason to fear for her life. She noted that the bystanders took part in adding "to the power of the bully by not intervening. The second sentenced girl had taken part in the final phone call, however there was no evidence the girl had broken the law.

Cindy Wesley, mother of Dawn Marie, requested that the convicted girl be sentenced using an aboriginal sentencing circle. She wanted to honor the memory of her daughter's partial aboriginal history, as well as that of the offender. All parties to the action agreed. Dawn-Marie's mom wanted a chance to speak with the teenager and her family.

During the sentencing circle the teen took the ceremonial eagle feather twice and tried to speak. She broke down each time and was urged by Cindy Wesley to try again. The teen was ultimately able to apologize. The offender's family hopes the case will keep other girls from making the same mistake. They hope that the sentencing circle process will set the offender on the right track.

The offender received 18 months probation with terms including no use of alcohol or drugs, random drug testing, counseling and anger management and a prohibition on cell phone use. She needed to write a 750 word essay on bullying and complete 20 hours of community service as well.

A documentary has been made called "Rats & Bullies", which tells Dawn-Marie's story and explores the unique characteristics of female bullying while offering methods of bullying prevention.

Emmet Fralick

In April of 2002, in Halifax, Emmet Fralick, a 14 year old grade 9 student, couldn't take the abuse anymore. Emmet was being harassed by peers at his school.

A group of teenagers, led by a 15 year old girl, made demands on Emmet, including giving them $40 each day. When Emmet wasn't able to come up with the money, he was put in a circle and forced to choose which one of his peers would beat him up that day. He was punched, kicked, burned with cigarettes and forced to eat dog feces. He had been given a broken nose, black eyes and a broken thumb through these abuses.

Emmet was afraid to tell those who cared what was happening. He would lie about his bruises, or hide them. He sold everything he owned to try to pay the bullies. He was caught shoplifting, as he was attempting to steal things he could sell to get the money. Emmet's friends knew what he was experiencing and would sometimes give him money, but all the children were too afraid to tell an adult what was happening.

Bullying continued in the school after Fralick committed suicide, but students began to ask for more help. Students said "Because this whole thing happened, no one's going to take anything from anyone anymore." and "If anything good came out of the suicide, it was the fact that it brought the problem forward."

Emmet Fralick's parents urge other parents to be involved in their children's lives and to try to be aware of what's happening for their children. The following words come from Emmet's mom, Lois:

"I did not know my son Emmet was being bullied until after his suicide. I believe everyone has a purpose in life, and Emmett's purpose was to open our eyes to bullying. Let's not waste Emmet's purpose by pretending that bullying isn't happening or it is not important, let's come up with solutions to the problem."

One girl in this case was charged with extortion, assault and threat to cause bodily harm. She was sentenced to one year in youth jail. The same girl has pleaded guilty to three other charges stemming from another case of bullying.

When Your Child is Using Bully Actions

When you see or hear that your child is using bullying actions with other children, you must create expectations that will stop the behavior, and examine your own actions.

1. Do you laugh at or mock others in your child's presence? Even in what might seem like small ways to you?
2. Do you make derogatory jokes that others sometimes don't appreciate?
3. Do you engage in, or talk about physical violence as a resolution tactic?
4. Do you engage in, or talk about revenge tactics?
5. Do you display disrespect for other people?
6. Do you send messages to your child that fighting means you are strong or tough?

If you don't see these qualities in yourself, look for someone else that your child may be imitating. If your child is clearly imitating another guardian, relative or friend, address that situation directly. Pay attention to your child's screen time. What are they playing on the computer or gaming system? What are they watching on tv? This influences their behavior. I remember so well, a phrase from a youth camp I attended long ago. "Garbage in, garbage out." We create our own lives, and part of how we do that is through outside influence. Outside influence creates thought patterns. Thought patterns create actions...you see the connection.

Set your standards high for how you and your child will treat people, and be consistent with both expectations and discipline when your child treats people disrespectfully.

The bullying definition provided here can help you to evaluate your child's behavior, and the questions above can be answered by your child as well as yourself. Some children are more naturally empathetic to others and are able to clearly understand what hurts and what doesn't. Other children must be more clearly taught how their behavior affects others.

If your child manages Attention Deficit Hyperactivity Disorder (ADHD/ADD) or Fetal Alcohol Spectrum Disorder, or another barrier, they may be in the category of needing direct teaching about how their behavior affects others. They also require consistency in expectations – as do all children.

When Your Child is Using Victim Responses

When your child is using victim responses, you are likely to see fear of other students, low self confidence and a great deal of negative self-talk. You may see your child believing what another child is saying, or withdrawing from peers. Your child may have a heightened fight or flight response, and be in a cycle of detrimental habits, including poor nutrition and lack of exercise/physical strength. There may be heightened negative perceptions of their physical self.

Bullying is not a one-time event for most children. They will experience various bullying behavior throughout their young lives. Since their self-confidence and communication skills are critical to overcoming bully actions, the strategies offered here are intended as long-term solutions to help kids grow in these areas. Children who can communicate well, and understand themselves and others are less likely to be bullied and are more likely to judge and describe events as they are happening. They are also less likely to engage in bullying behavior themselves.

Parents and teachers alike find it difficult to decide whether to intervene in bullying situations. Though parents will express dismay over the treatment of their children, they aren't sure what to do. Children will sometimes express these struggles to their parents, and still ask their parents not to become involved, thus leaving parents helpless and confused. When your child does not want you to become actively involved in the situation it becomes necessary to find behind-the-scene ways to help. This material helps you with that, allowing you to coach your child from the sidelines and help your child grow.

When Your Child is a Bystander

This is the opportunity every parent has to give their child information. Because even if you can't identify that your child is using bully actions, and even if your child has never made a disclosure that they are being bullied, you can approach them as if they are a bystander. The majority of children are or will be bystanders at some point in time.

The bystander role is the most important in the bullying cycle. While it might seem almost irrelevant, it has been shown to be the most effective strategy to change the culture of bullying. This only makes sense. Schools that are at risk need change. They need peaceful revolution that involves understanding each other, developing empathy and the decomposition of existing unhealthy cliques. This is where bystanders come in. Someone using bully actions isn't going to start the peaceful revolution. Someone experiencing bully actions isn't likely to be able to start the peaceful revolution. That is the role of the bystander.

Bystanders need all the same skills that children using bully actions and victim responses need. They need to be able to balance and understand their own thinking, and the thinking of others, develop empathy, and become strong communicators.

Self Esteem

There is a lot of talk about whether children who are frequently using bully actions have low self esteem or high self esteem.

We believe that either one of these may be the case. A child that frequently uses bully actions may be living in a lifestyle of bullying. He may be bullied, leading to low self esteem, building of esteem through anger and aggressive action, and retaliation. A child may also have extremely high self esteem, seeing other people as present to serve his ultimate purpose. He may view others with contempt, and may come from a family who is contemptuous of others.

Either way, a child frequently using bully actions, needs to learn to understand others, understand themselves, feel and show empathy, communicate well, and understand the consequences to others of using the actions. Role models need to examine the messages they are sending, even if it seems like the messages are being sent in a small way.

Teaching Points For Your Child

1. **True bullying feeds on the fear of others.** Teach your child how to minimize their fight or flight response in order to appear calm to one who is using bully actions. This is taught through breathing and relaxation exercises. When you are aware of how to relax yourself you are able to manage every

situation that presents itself in a more positive fashion.

2. **Bullying behavior by other children is a chance for your child to grow.** Rather than acting simply in a protective role, teach your child how to manage the situation for himself. Bullying behavior exists in both schools and workplaces. The time to bully-proof your child from workplace bullying actions is now.

3. **Bullying behavior is unacceptable coming from YOU and your child.** Point out behavior that you see as being inappropriate or hurtful to others. Allow your child to see you acting in positive ways towards others, and when you do hurt someone, allow them to know or see that you apologize, and that you work to heal with those that you have harmed.

4. **Your child will increase in self-confidence by practicing and managing bullying behavior.** Role-playing can help your child try out potential approaches. Have your child act the part of the child using a bully action while you respond. Then you act the part of the bully action, allowing your child a chance to respond. Involve another person and take turns playing the bystander.

Child	(Hits parent) Gimme your lunch!
Parent	(Stepping back) Forget it!

Other options:
- Moving to a location where adults are watching (review such locations with the child)
- Respond with assertive phrases
- Respond with humor
- Team up with peers
- Respond with extra kindness
- Respond with silence, a steely glare and a relaxed body

5. **Work with your child to increase self -confidence and self-esteem in general.** This happens actively as well as through role-modeling. Don't speak negatively about yourself. If you use terms such as "I'm a loser," when you make a mistake, your child learns HE is a loser when he makes a mistake. When you or your child make a mistake, turn it around and seek the learning experience from it. Teach your child the purpose of mistakes and failures is to do better the next time. Teach your child to notice, identify and value his own positive qualities as well as those of others.

6. **Give your child affirming messages.** If you say to your child "You are a pushover," your child begins to define himself in that way. Turn it around and say instead, "I know you'll be able to stand up for yourself." Speak out loud the positives you see in your child. This will help your children define themselves in these positive ways, giving them strength to manage whatever situations may arise.

7. **Teach your child that facing their fears increases confidence.** Again, check your own role-modeling. Do you avoid problems?

8. **Avoid the temptation of telling your child to return the bullying with physical violence.** For most children this advice is unhelpful and simply reinforces a belief that personal power comes from violence-related strength.

9. **Teach your child to use humour as a tool.** A snappy comeback can diffuse conflict situations and create a more positive method of personal power. This only works if it is suited to your child's personality.

10. **Bully actors seek children they can scare.** To bully-proof your children you must help them to respond

in ways that discourage further bullying action against them.

11. **Teach your children to recognize inaccurate thinking.** Explain to them that we all have thoughts about ourselves, others and the world that aren't quite right, and that we must challenge those thoughts.

Role-Playing

Role-playing is one of the most effective tools for teaching children how to manage bully actions and victim responses. This type of change management allows a child to control the situation and to learn, through practice, the exact thing they need. Role playing may be used in schools and in families, and is an effective tool to teach skills that overcome both bully actions and victim responses.

Role-playing allows us to examine roles we're not used to, and practice responses that we'll use later. Thinking ahead outside our comfort zone, allows us to experiment, or improvise – instead of simply reacting to situations.

Although there are a number of techniques you can use to facilitate role-playing, some of the best involve improvisation, in which you don't use a formal script.

Discuss your child's situation with them to determine your child's needs. This also provides opportunity for the development of a closer relationship and better understanding of your child's day to day experiences.

Brainstorming

Brainstorming is the process of generating as many ideas as possible in a given (usually short and fixed) time. It may be ineffective if some of these are true:
- the solution to your problem is clear,
- everybody agrees on what to do,
- either it's a really simple problem, or only the teacher can fix things.

With difficult problems, there is a temptation to take a limited view of possible solution methods, or even to throw up your hands and give up. If this is likely, of course brainstorming will not help at all.

In difficult situations, establish a list of needs prior to beginning brainstorming. The list of needs can begin the idea creation and can also become a measuring stick against which to measure if ideas will work or not, when the brainstorming exercise is complete. Simply ask the question, does this idea meet the needs?

In terms of brainstorming solutions to bullying with your child, some ideas to consider are: the need for safety, the need to change the situation, the need to provide protection to someone else (bystander), the need for prevention of further bullying.

There is a strong temptation to criticize "bad ideas." Everyone involved in the brainstorming exercise must agree in advance to avoid this, or not participate. The brainstorming process is brief; there's no time for distractions. Even if "bad ideas" are a distraction, discussing or criticizing ideas is worse.

After the brainstorming period is over, there'll be time enough for

- eliminating irrelevant ideas
- grouping similar or related ideas
- commenting and modifying incomplete ideas
- ranking whatever ideas remain
- discussing if the ideas match the needs listed
-

...but that's a separate process. In the meantime, establish ground rules before you start:

- The group has one leader.
- The leader's only purpose is to keep things moving.

- The problem to be addressed is clearly understood by the entire group.
- Everyone has a chance to contribute. You can go around the table to solicit ideas, but this can pressure those who don't feel comfortable speaking up; on the other hand, if ideas are taken freestyle, vocal members of the group can dominate.
- Every contribution should be in that person's own words.
- No idea is criticized.
- The group has one recorder. You can have the recorder write everything on a board or flipchart, which would be easy for all to read; on the other hand, collecting Post-It Notes from each member of the group is easier on the recorder. Either way, it's important for the ideas to be in one place, where they can lead to more ideas.

Understanding and using the brainstorming process allows children to have a tool that they can use to gather and evaluate ideas during difficult periods of time in their lives.

Pledging

Working with your child to prevent bullying issues is ongoing. Consider taking a pledge with your child, to show each of your commitment to each other, and to learning through difficulties during these school years. For examples of pledges that you can print and sign with your child, go to http://nosuchthingasabully.com .

Protection Lessons for Parents and Children

Goals

We're going to take a moment to work together to set your goals. Imagine being asked these questions, and answer them for yourself as honestly as possible:

What are the troublesome behaviors you see your child use?
Who are the influential people in your child's life?
How do they, and you, influence your child's behavior?
What do you want to have happen from using these lessons?

Self Assessment of your own communication style:

Think about the following questions. Consider if you act different ways with different people.

When a person finishes a conversation with me, does it seem like they feel respected? Do I feel good?

(If so, you are likely communicating assertively. You are treating both others and yourself with respect. This type of behavior creates strong relationships and puts children in a good position to be positive bystanders.)

Am I forceful with other people? Do I yell? Glare? Use other angry body language? Do I intimidate other people?

(If so, you are likely communicating aggressively. This type of behavior models and encourages bullying behavior in children.)

Do I feel like I have been respectful to myself and my own needs? Am I doing things I don't want to do or am not comfortable with? Am I afraid, or do I find it awkward to say no?

(If so, you are likely communicating passively. This type of behavior can teach children to follow other children even if they are not comfortable with what is happening.)

Do I do things for others and take care of them, without taking care of myself? Am I more worried about everyone else being okay than I am about myself being okay? Do I occasionally explode in anger? Do I refrain from telling others exactly what I think, but talk about it with others afterwards?

(If so, you are likely communicating passively aggressively. This type of behavior doesn't teach children to set boundaries, or control their temper. They may be susceptible to bullying or conflicts with friends, or to becoming extremely stressed themselves.)

Reminders of the four communication types follow. Remember that you may use different types of behavior in different situations and with different people:

Assertive: When you are assertive, you are respectful to yourself and to others. You meet your own needs while still being aware of the needs and feelings of others. You know that there are human rights and responsibilities that you must live by, such as the right to say no and the responsibility to do so clearly. You are aware that others have the same rights and responsibilities. You are able to speak out in order to meet your needs and you can do so in a way that is respectful of other people. You deal with a conflict in a way that is respectful to all involved. You try to understand where others are coming from and work towards resolution that is fair to all the players involved.

Passive: When you are passive, you are more respectful of other people than of yourself. You do not act directly to meet your own needs. You feel uncomfortable about coming right out and saying no. You feel that others take advantage of you, and you have trouble standing up for yourself. You go with the flow, even if you are unhappy about where the flow is taking you. You are sometimes described as a "doormat," because people "walk all over you." You will often choose to walk away from a conflict. You tend to withdraw, may have difficulty saying no and may have trouble making eye contact. You act in ways that smooth the waters. Your preference is to keep things calm rather than to meet your own needs. The result can be bitterness, unhappiness and a sense of others' taking advantage of your "niceness."

Aggressive: When you are aggressive you are more respectful to yourself than to other people. Using your aggressive behavior, you try to meet your own needs, but you do so at the expense of others. Others are harmed, either emotionally or physically by you. You will meet a conflict head on, using emotional, verbal or physical force to get your needs met. You don't worry about the needs of others. Sometimes you yell, threaten, and use frightening body language.

Passive-aggressive: When you are passive aggressive, you are not being respectful to anyone. You might be mostly passive, leading to a build up of resentments until you become aggressive and blow up. You are unwilling to approach people with whom you are angry, but you talk behind their backs. You might even start rumors or seek ways to "get even." You are taking out aggression, but at a distance from the perceived offenders.

It is important to be aware of your communication and thought patterns, and the ways in which those have been passed on to your children. Keep in mind that this is about assessing, not judging. It is easier for children to become more assertive if their parents demonstrate assertive behavior. No parents, even the really, really good ones, are perfect. This isn't about measuring how bad you've been, it's about looking at places where you would like to be better.

Protection One: Conflict vs. Bullying

It is important for you to accept your child's perception of a situation and to try to understand the situation and its Importance to your child. At times, the conflicts that children experience can seem small and are easily dismissed by busy parents. It may only be after repeated reporting that an adult identifies the situation as bullying.

You must listen to what your child is saying and monitor their experiences. You can start coaching your child very early by giving bully actions such as hitting, or taking, consistent treatment. You can model and practice appropriate reactions with your child when they are on the receiving end of bully actions. You can start explaining to your child when they have to tell – when your child, or someone else is in trouble and telling will get them out of trouble, or when someone might be hurt if they don't tell.

Keep in mind that these small conflicts are training grounds for children to learn the communication and problem solving skills that they will need as they grow. It is important not to take over their small conflicts. Instead, you must let them learn from them. But you must also keep them safe, so it is important to stay aware.

Activities:

Brainstorm examples of bully actions with your child. This is also nicely done with a group of siblings.

Brainstorm examples of disagreements with friends. Discuss if these are bullying. Why? Why not? Ask if there are power imbalances between the friends.

If they get stuck, help them along with questions. Don't come up with their answers for them. Do ask questions that are relevant to their lives. Ask about interactions with specific friends, or at specific places.

Example questions to assist with the brainstorming exercise include:

- Do you see any fighting at school? Are you involved in any fighting at school?

- Do you ever argue with your friends?

- When do you feel angry?

Create a story with your child. Use the following guidelines.

- Make sure the story contains some of the discussion from the brainstorming session.

- You add a few sentences, then your child adds a few sentences.

- Writing the story down creates a memory and also an extra imprint of the information for both of you. It solidifies the issues that you are working to manage.

Start practicing role playing with your child. Switch roles, with each person playing the child using the bully action, the child using the victim response, and a bystander. Use the examples you have created, or use these examples:

- Some children are playing a rowdy sports game. One boy is continuously way too rough.

- Two children are talking. One wants to go to the movie, the other wants to go to the baseball game. One child pushes the other.

- Tommy has borrowed a personal music player from his friend Tina. He has broken the player. Tina is yelling at Tommy.

Use the bullying definition to evaluate the situations and see if bullying actions are being used. If you need more information about the bullying definition first, skip ahead and read Lesson 10.

Have your child create a story about bullying or an argument happening to a made-up child. If this will be a chore, omit it. It is important that your child not feel this is extra homework!

If you or your child enjoys artwork, draw with them as you have this conversation. Or if your child is smaller and you like to draw, draw simple pictures that reflect the conversation and have your child color them in.

Invite your child to start a private journal, at this point. Tell them they are always welcome to share it with you, but the main part of having a journal is to learn to use it to figure out your thinking and your problems, and to write about good things. Again, if your child finds this a chore, omit it – but a pleasant shopping trip for a nice book and fun pen to use for journaling can improve the chances of your child learning to use this valuable tool!

Protection Two: Feelings

As adults, we have learned to deny many feelings. We have learned to hide them – or they have warped into something else, most likely anger. As a part of facilitating this process for your child, you are going to have to be in touch with your own feelings. You must understand a few things about feelings.

First of all, ANGER is a secondary emotion. We show, and express anger in conjunction with another emotion, one that society has labeled as a 'weaker' emotion. Humiliation, confusion, frustration, sadness, distress, betrayal, helplessness, fear...these are the emotions that adults often refuse to let themselves express – even to themselves.

The refusal to express these emotions is something that is learned. If we are left in a natural state, never having any traumas, never having anyone try to change our personalities (through threats like, "I'll give you something to cry about!"), then we would be likely to have no problem at all expressing these emotions.

Life gets in the way though. You might have had parents who wanted you to toughen up. You might have had experiences that caused you to have to create a shell. You might have such strong feelings that even the thought of trying to figure them out is distressing. You might even think about closing this book right now. Please don't.

In order to resolve anger, emotions underneath anger must be addressed. You don't have to entirely figure out your own emotions in order to help your child, but it will definitely help you with your journey.

Even if you don't understand your child's feelings, you must accept them. If you don't accept them, your child will stop telling you about them, possibly learning to bottle emotions, resulting in anger. Anger blocks positive relationships and creates inaccurate thinking.

Figuring out how you are feeling is difficult, both for adults and children. There is a list of feeling words at http://nosuchthingasabully.com . Use the words provided to help you. Don't let this difficulty block you or your child from pursuing this important basic ability.

All humans have a basic fight or flight response when feeling threatened. A sense of threat can come from any negative emotion. When your body goes into fight or flight response, there is an increase in the amount of adrenaline that is pumped through your body. This causes a variety of changes! Your heart rate increases, the oxygen to your brain decreases (some people even see red), and your decision making is impaired. More blood and oxygen are transported to the large muscles, which will be used to fight or run. All those silly exercises, count to ten, take deep breaths, walk around the block... those are intended to get the oxygen back in your brain before you say (or do) something you regret.

Expect to be uncomfortable with some of your child's feelings. Again, acceptance is important. If some of the emotions that come up are about you, take a moment to examine your fight or flight response, and refrain from becoming defensive. This is very important.

People can feel many emotions at the same time, including ones that would seem very contradictory.

When a child is in tune with his own feelings, he is more likely to be aware of the feelings of other people. Children need to understand that all human beings have the same kinds of emotions. Growth of empathy starts when you start teaching your child to understand his own feelings and the feelings of others.

Activities:

In order to lesson the pressure of opening up with your own and your child's feelings, use other scenarios to identify how other people are feeling.

Jill's parents are getting divorced. She is also having trouble with a boy at school who keeps on pestering her. Sometimes he pinches and hits her too. She doesn't know what to do. How do you think Jill is feeling?

Tom and James have been friends since kindergarten. They have argued and are angry with one another. They have said they won't be hanging out anymore. How do you think Tom and James are feeling?

Sally is on her way to a friend's party. Her parents were arguing last night. She had a pretty good day in school, but didn't do as well on a test as she had hoped. How is Sally feeling?

You get caught up with a group of friends who are making fun of someone else. How is the person who is being made fun of feeling? How do you feel?

Read any book or passage that names several emotions. Talk with your child about the feelings mentioned in the book.

Print the list of feeling words on the No Such Thing as a Bully website. Using the list, make slips of paper with the words printed on them. Group the words into emotions that are similar. Group the words into emotions that you might feel at the same time. Use the words to play "emotions" charades. Use the list as you discuss the scenarios above as well.

Using magnetic letters, express today's feelings on the refrigerator. Large families may wish to color code for each child. This is a great activity for adults to join in as well. Children need to learn that EVERYONE has feelings!

Alternatively, draw expressive faces with your children for the family to choose from to post on the fridge or a bulletin board.

Protection Three: Fight, Flight or Freeze

We touched briefly on the fight or flight response in the context of helping your child begin to understand and talk about their emotions. This lesson explores the fight or flight response further, adding the element of "freeze".

The symptoms of a fight or flight response are as follows:

- increased heart rate
- upset or butterfly stomach
- tense muscles
- fast, sometimes regrettable verbal or physical reactions
- quick thoughts/seeing red

For some people, the response includes freezing of thought and/or physical abilities.

Think about times when you have experienced a fight or flight reaction. What are the things that set you into a fight or flight reaction? What are the situations or phrases that you find threatening? Often, especially with regard to parenting, a threat to parental authority (a child talking back) will cause a fight or flight reaction.

Again, in combination with the fight or flight reaction, remember that anger has an underlying emotion. To dissolve a reaction, the underlying emotion and threat must be recognized. Once it is, it can be addressed and removed. Remaining adrenaline can be removed through physical activity and relaxation practice.

Dissolving this reaction is essential to becoming more assertive. Becoming more assertive helps you, and your child manage others' bad behavior in a calm and capable way.

Activities:

Explain the fight or flight response, and adrenaline to your child.

Brainstorm how you and your child are affected by fight or flight reactions. Discuss what kinds of things bring on fight or flight reactions for each of you (keeping it child appropriate – do not discuss work conflict or conflict with your spouse), and how that reaction feels.

Take your pulse, teaching your child how to do the same and helping them. Run in place for a minute. Take your pulse/child's pulse again. Talk about how an elevated heart rate feels. Talk about the difference between elevating your heart through exercise versus the fight or flight reaction. What are the differences in how your body feels?

Brainstorm and practice activities your child likes that use up extra adrenaline.

Lie down and practice breathing deeply together. Try to time your breathing to your child's breathing to make it comfortable for your child. Put your hand on your stomach, and on your child's stomach to show how, when you breathe in, your stomach expands. Depending on the age of your child and the relationship you have with them, you may wish to have them lay their head on your stomach and feel the motion that happens when you breathe deeply.

Explore age appropriate meditation tapes with your child. Examples are found on the *No Such Thing as a Bully*® website.

There is a two minute relaxation exercise on the *No Such Thing as a Bully*® website. Follow the instructions and practice the exercise together.

Role-play threatening situations. These may be bullying situations, or dinosaur attacks or any other situation that your child is interested in. Mirror some of the stories discussed in previous lessons, particularly for older children. After the role-play, ask them to describe how they feel. Is their heart going faster? Are they sweating?

Notice your own fight flight and freeze reactions and those of your child in the weeks and months to come.

Protection Four: Important Ideas

There are some basic principles of communication that tend to build positive relationships.

Idea One

Good communication skills help you to stand up for yourself. They also help you to avoid and resolve conflict.

If you, and your child are able to communicate well, you will have less conflict throughout your lives. When conflict arises, you will be better equipped to handle it. When people use bully actions, you will have more tools to be able to deflect them.

Idea Two

Conflict and bullying are two different things. Conflict is found in many everyday situations, and can help your child to learn. Being able to distinguish between conflict and bullying is important.

Idea Three

Everyone is going to have a different perception. Every story has several sides to it. Trying to understand perceptions can help to increase empathy in children.

Remember that your child, regardless of age, is not going to have the same perceptions as you, even while experiencing a common situation.

Idea Four

The fight or flight reaction is natural but you can learn more balanced ways of approaching threats.

You can keep your own reaction and other people's reactions in mind when you are dealing with conflict, or even with bullying. You can use relaxation techniques and balanced thinking strategies to control your own reactions.

You can learn to moderate your approach so that you can help other people keep their reactions down too.

Idea Five

Most people do not want to escalate problems but they do not have an understanding of positive approaches or conflict minimization strategies.

When you are trying to deal with a bullying situation, keep in mind that you might be better able to communicate about the problem than the other guy. The other parents, teachers, principals, school boards – they may all experience a fight or flight reaction in hearing about your child's issue. Remember to help the other guy out by staying calm and providing some ideas for solutions.

Idea Six

Be aware of your personal reactions. You must be aware of what causes you to react. For some people it is being called a certain name. For others it is seeing someone else being hurt. During certain times in your life you are under more stress than others, which affects your personal reactions. Know and examine your reactions in order to learn more about yourself.

Idea Seven

If you understand that people have different perceptions, open discussion will result in genuine and often unique solutions.

Even when bullying is severe and when it is based in contempt, open discussion is necessary. There needs to be an understanding of what happened from each person's point of view. A person who is contemptuous learns to be empathetic by understanding the emotions and situations of others. Speaking openly about conflict can help you understand the perception of the other person. Be open to receiving this information, rather than feeling threatened because your perceptions differ. This shift in understanding opens up the discussion and moves the conflict forward so you can brainstorm solutions that will best meet the needs of everyone.

Activities:

Explain the ideas to your child at their level. The following alternate explanations may help.

- We both have to make sure we have the words and ideas to respond to bullying. Being assertive will keep you from using bully actions or victim responses.

- Bullying and conflict are two different things. It is important to know the difference between the two.

- People must understand each others perceptions and how they see the world.

- You have a fight or flee reaction when you feel threatened... So does the other guy!

- Having ideas and words to stand up to bullying peacefully is important. Share your ideas.

- It is important to know about yourself, to know when you feel angry and when you feel sad. If you know how you feel, it's easier to tell others what you need.

- Talking about problems will help you to solve them. It helps you understand the other guy, and get rid of assumptions. You must know how to listen.

Discuss the fight or flight reaction again, talking about the lesson that you used previously.

Discuss assumptions. Discuss the question, "Do you know this for sure?" This is best done through natural conversation. Talk about times that you made assumptions and were wrong. Help your child find times that he did the same.

Talk about listening. Be completely silent for a short period of time. Then talk about what you hear when you are listening, instead of making noise.

Talk openly about your child's perception of differences in the lifestyles they see around them. They may know children with one or two parents, they may know children from different cultures. Discuss differences, placing value on everyone.

Practice finding out about "someone" with your child, through role play. Ask your child to make up a person. She doesn't have to have all the details in mind. Now, you ask open questions of your child as that person. Find out as much as you can about the pretend person. Switch roles after 10 minutes or when you run out of questions and answers. Reverse roles. Lesson 14 contains information about types of questions, and may be reviewed before this activity.

Have your child practice finding out about and understanding other family members and friends. This almost becomes an interview process, but what it does is two pronged. Your child learns how to learn about someone – and learning about someone is a very important friendship skill.

Protection Five: The Bullying Spiral

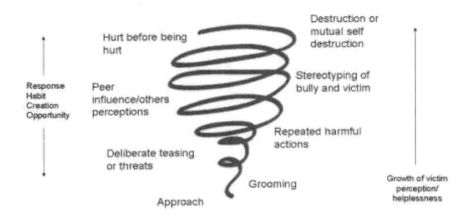

You've seen this before, but you have to now help your child understand, how bullying develops and the points in time when it can be stopped.

One person is approached by another person. If the approaching person has learned to control by power, the grooming pattern includes testing; How will this person react to me?

STOPPER: You need to be able to set boundaries right here. If the approaching person sees that he cannot control another, the testing is not successful. Being able to stand up for yourself and others, starts here. A lot of bully actions can be prevented when you are able to do this.

If the approaching person feels he CAN have some power over the other person, the teasing, threats and/or harmful actions continue and accelerate as long as the situation is not addressed, and the victim responses are continuing.

STOPPER: Your child must know that you are prepared to listen and help if he tells you he is repeatedly experiencing bully actions at the hands of his peers. Encourage your child to TELL if he or someone else is being repeatedly bullied.

Peer influences play a very big part in the bullying spiral. Peer influences can directly affect whether or not bullying will continue. If bullying is supported by peers cheering it on, or even just trying to ignore it, it is likely to continue. It has been shown that a child using bully actions will reconsider their use if the actions are not supported by their peers and/or if they are not getting the reaction they are seeking over a period of time.

STOPPER: Your child needs to understand how very important it is for them to step up for another child when they see bully actions happening. They need to understand how to become friends with others, both so that they have a positive support group and so that others do.

Players in the scenario may be characterized as a bully and a victim. If this has happened for your child, their self concept may begin to develop around that negative label.

STOPPER: Reassure your child that bully actions and victim responses are simply behaviors that get used. Every person has the power to use different behaviors. Work together to practice using different, better behaviors.

The child using victim responses is likely to feel helpless and may lash out at others. As they define themselves as a victim, their behavior becomes habit. The child using bully actions may feel helpless to change their behavior. They make a lot of sacrifices in terms of peer group status if they change their behavior. As they define themselves as a bully, their behavior becomes a habit.

STOPPER: Pay attention to your child's behaviors, and work with them to replace behaviors with assertive behavior, develop empathy if needed, strengthen a positive self-concept, and enhance friendship skills. Address issues with peers and provide opportunities for introduction to new peer groups.

At the height of the spiral, destruction or mutual self destruction may result. This can even be an automatic stress responses, such as a person who is bullied snapping and physically hurting someone. This happened in the case of Ritchard Gale and Casey Heynis. Another scenario includes children who feel they have been victimized making plans for revenge on a grand scale, such as in Columbine. Suicide, is another method of destruction which impacts those who have used bully actions. In some situations, people have been charged and convicted for bully actions leading to someone's suicide. There is no good stopper here. We must stop the spiral before this point.

Activities:

Use the explanation above to explain the Bullying Spiral to your child.

Brainstorm and discuss real life bullying situations that escalated. Do some internet research. Describe how they might have gone through these processes. Go to http://nosuchthingasabully.com for a list of links to assist you in getting started.

Role play a bullying situation with three or more people. Have one or more people stand up for the person who is being bullied. Talk about how that affects the situation.

Roleplay a bullying situation where your child is alone. Have your child practice standing up for himself. Reverse the roles and keep practicing.

Go to http://nosuchthingasabully.com for a homemade sticks and buttons race activity about good and bad friendship qualities!

Protection Six: Working Through Harm

Knowing how and when to say you are sorry, and MEANING it is tremendously important. There are essentially two ways to come to repentance. A person can get caught, and feel sorry they've been caught. This repentance is self-centered and tends to be less effective in the long term. It is not based in understanding. It is important to try to move from self-centered repentance to other-centered repentance. This happens when you accept your own behavior and begin to understand the other person, and why what you've done is hurtful.

The second way of coming to repentance is feeling sorry that you have been involved in something that has hurt someone else. A person feeling this other-centered repentance is able to quickly identify when they need to apologize, and mean it. A person feeling other-centered repentance is more likely to be able to work through "the three R's"[8], restitution, resolution and reconciliation.

When your child is involved in bullying situations, whether as the primary child using bully actions, or as one who has been co-opted to support the bully, you must help them to understand how their action has affected the other person, and regardless of whether or not they acknowledge the hurt they have caused, they must still work through the consequential three R's.

Repentance will often lead to an apology, but without sincerity <u>and</u> a change in behavior, apologies are not terribly helpful. Restitution, resolution and reconciliation may lead to sincere repentance. The following descriptions of the three R's, and how to facilitate them are based in

---

[8] Barbara Coloroso, The Bully, The Bullied and The Bystander, 2004

Barbara Coloroso's work in "The Bully, The Bullied and The Bystander"[9].

1. Restitution: This means fixing the problem that has been created. If an item has been damaged, it must be replaced, if damaging rumors have been spread, the offender must step up and admit to spreading untrue rumors. Physical harm is more difficult to fix, and the regaining of trust is a process that takes time. Trust is earned over a period of time of changed behavior.

2. Resolution: This means preventing another incident from happening. There are three steps to this, accepting what happened, understanding why it happened and your own emotions around it, and learning something positive from it.

3. Reconciliation: This is the process of healing alongside the person you have hurt. Because safety of the person who has been harmed is so important, they cannot be forced to be involved in a reconciliation process. This does not preclude a reconciliation process for the other child. A great question to ask is "What can I do to help the person I have hurt have a better time?" or "What can I do to help other people in general?" Coloroso identifies that this helps a child to "be good and do good", providing an opportunity that is the antithesis to bullying actions.

---

[9] Barbara Coloroso, The Bully, The Bullied and The Bystander, 2004.

To gain a fuller understanding and for ideas about how this could be applied to situations currently in the media, go to http://nosuchthingasabully.com .

When your child has used a bully action, working through this process allows your child to understand that he is just a person who did something wrong, and can fix what he has done wrong. It is not WHO he is, rather, it is simply what he has done and can repair.

Something to note, is that when you are in a situation where you are working well with the other guy, and you are creating the opportunity to be involved in good works, a Serotonin Response is created. Basically, instead of producing a lot of fight or flight adrenaline, the body is increasing its production of serotonin, the feel good hormone that keeps us from falling into a depression.

Bringing this down to a level for younger children means that you parent consistently, and use the three R's with your children when you see bully actions. They still must go through three steps, and work through them with your help.

1. How can you fix this?
2. How can you stop this from happening again?
3. What can you do that is being good and doing good and helping someone else?

Activities:

Use the explanation above to explain the steps to your child. Ask your child if there was a time when they did something wrong and felt sorry right away. What happened? Did they apologize? Did they change the behavior? Tell your child about a time when you did.

To see how this fits with current situations in the media, go to http://nosuchthingasabully.com .

Work through the following scenarios that use bully actions to their logical end point, using the three R's.

Samantha and Julie have been good friends. Lately Samantha has been hanging around with some other girls and sometimes she treats Julie meanly. Lately she has been verbally 'teasing' Julie about her clothes. Julie feels excluded and hurt. Lately, Samantha's friends have posted men comments to Julie's Facebook page.

Questions to ask:
How responsible is Samantha for the situation? Her new friends?
How can Samantha work through restitution? How can she fix this?
How can Samantha work through resolution? How can Samantha make sure she isn't involved in this kind of behavior again?
How can Samantha work through reconciliation? What can she do to make things better for Julie?

John has been using bullying behaviors for a long time, and a lot of children are afraid of him. He has a big following, and seems popular, because no one wants to cross him and become one of his targets. Finally, a small group of children have decided to group together and tell an adult what is happening.

How can adults help John work through the three R's?
How responsible is John for the situation?
How can he work through restitution? How can he fix this?
How can John work through resolution? How can John make sure he stops using bully actions?

How can John work through reconciliation? What can he do to make things better for kids at school, and for other people?

How can John understand the point of view of the people affected by his bully actions?

Do you think that John will feel sorry for his actions when he works through the three R's?

Mandy and Kyle are friends, and they both like each other. Mandy gets invited to a party that Kyle is not invited to, and she really wants to go. She lies to Kyle about it and says she is doing something with her family. Kyle phones her that night and catches her in a lie.

This is a little more complicated! Some questions:

Is this a bully action? Check the definition again and see if it fits. If it doesn't fit, can the three R's still be used?

Why do you think Mandy lied? How do you think she might feel? How do you think Kyle might feel?

How can Mandy work through restitution? How can she fix this?

How can Mandy work through resolution? How can Mandy make sure she stops using that type of behavior?

How can Mandy work through reconciliation? Do you think Kyle will be willing to work through it with her? What can she do to make things better for Kyle?

Protection Seven: How You Act

Aggressive: You have respect for your own needs, but not for the needs of others. You are likely to be at risk of using bully actions. Examples: yelling, namecalling, hitting, threatening, belittling

Passive: You respect the needs of others, but not your own. You may be at risk to be a 'doormat', and to using victim responses. Examples: going along with the group, even if the group is going against what you want; saying yes when you would rather say no.

Passive Aggressive: You don't respect yourself, or others. You may use bully actions sometimes and victim responses other times. Examples: being nice to someone to their face, but mean behind their back; doing a lot for someone and then blowing up instead of just saying no.

Assertive: You are respectful of yourself and others. You speak your mind clearly and respectfully. You are unlikely to use bully actions or victim responses. Examples: speaking up respectfully right away when someone treats you badly; saying no when you mean no and yes when you mean yes.

You've seen these before when you used the self assessment tool to determine how you use the behaviors. Anyone can use any of the behaviors in different situations. You might be passive with your children, and aggressive with your sister, or passive with your boss and aggressive with your children. Your behavior might fluctuate depending on mood and life circumstances. Being able to evaluate and understand your own behavior gives you power. Helping your child gain this skill involves him as part of his own life plan and gives him power. Having a sense of involvement and power in your life is one of the biggest self-esteem builders available, and building a positive self concept is an important part of bully proofing a child.

Understanding that these are BEHAVIORS, not PERSONALITIES, is important. If you see someone as 'aggressive', it will be hard to look at them in a positive manner. If you see someone as 'using aggressive behavior', your interactions are likely to end up being more positive.

Interestingly, it seems to be assertive behavior that increases a person's serotonin level the most, while the other behaviors increase adrenaline and encourage a fight or flight response.

Activities:

Identify that passive is often the same as "flight or freeze" and Aggressive is often the same as "fight" in the Fight, Flight or Freeze Response. When we flee from threats or conflict, we may do so by physically running away, but we may also do it by being fearful of saying no and letting people take advantage of us. When we fight against threats or conflict, we often use aggressive words or behaviors to display our fight reaction. We increase our adrenaline!

Look for examples of these types of behavior into the future, and directly point them out to your child. Also point out when your child seems to feel happy and remind them of the serotonin response. Help your child learn to notice and understand the connections between what they are doing and how they feel, particularly when the connections are positive. This helps develop your child's positive self concept and confidence. (If the relationship with your child is strained, be careful with this. Using the exercise to primarily identify negative behaviors will backfire, as will using it insincerely.)

Use the attached list of scenarios to help your child understand each type of behavior. Understanding what kind of behavior someone is using helps your child decide how to react. It allows your child to choose their reactions instead of simply reacting.

> Jed can be very loud. He'll often keep persuading and persuading until people do what he wants. Sometimes he threatens them, or gets mad and yells at them. People tend to try to avoid him although he has a group of friends that seem to stay the same. What kind of behavior is Jed using? (aggressive)

> Sandy thinks of himself as an easy going kind of guy. He just kind of tags along with his friends, and doesn't make too many demands about what he wants to do. One night Sandy and his friends end up at a party. They decide to go throw eggs at someone's house. Sandy tags along, but doesn't feel happy about what is happening. What kind of behavior is Sandy using? (passive)

> Praema has been helping her friend Brenna with homework. Lately Brenna is just expecting Praema to do it. Praema doesn't know how to tell her she isn't going to do it for her so she keeps on doing it. Finally Praema gets so angry that she ends the relationship with Brenna, but never tells her what is wrong. What kind of behavior is Praema using? (passive-aggressive)

Marie and Nancy have had an argument. Marie is very popular and has been spreading rumors about Nancy. She has also told her friends not to talk to Nancy at all. What kind of behavior is Marie using? (passive-aggressive)

Jonathan's parents are worried about him. Since changing to a bigger school, he has more friends that live farther away than before. His parents don't know where his friends live or even who many of them are. They want to give him stricter rules, and not let him go anywhere after school. Jonathan suggests that he write all the names of his friends and their addresses down for his parents and agrees to leave notes about where he is going, and phone and leave a message if he is somewhere else. His parents suggest having a small party where they could meet his new friends and then leave to a different part of the house, and just check in occasionally. What kind of behavior are Jonathan and his parents using? (assertive)

Do impromptu role-plays and help your child decide what kind of behavior was acted out. Here are some examples:

Two children are playing a game. One child is losing and throws the game board to the ground, waves his fist in the other's face, and stomps off. (Aggressive)

Jenna and Sara are walking down the street. Jenna wants to throw rocks at an old building. Sara says she doesn't want to, but Jenna doesn't listen. Sara ends up throwing the rocks too. (Passive)

Josh and Marie used to like each other. Now Marie is mad at Josh. Instead of talking to him about the problem, she is spreading bad rumors about him at school. (Passive Aggressive)

Ben and Arnie agreed to hang out on Saturday, but now they want to do different things. Ben wants to play video games, and Arnie wants to go for a bike ride. Arnie also wants Ben to help him deliver his papers. They talk about it and agree that they will deliver the papers using bikes, go for a ride, come back and play video games. (Assertive)

Protection Eight: Friendship Skills

Sometimes we make a wonderful friendship connection and the relationship is easy to maintain – essentially, we don't have to think very much about being that person's friend.

In life, though, situations arise where friendships can be more difficult. Children are thrown into situations where friendship skills are tremendously important. Particularly when they are experiencing bully actions against them, they may feel isolated and afraid. They may feel they have no outlet for their feelings, or that when they do try to express what is happening, they are ignored and further isolated. Children who are experiencing bully actions can alleviate some of their problems by learning strong friendship skills.

Often professionals talk about befriending the person using bully actions. That can be a solution, but it can also create a situation where a child has acquired a "friend" they are afraid to cross. It puts them at risk of becoming a user of bully actions. When it works in a balanced way, it can be a good thing. Otherwise, your child needs to know how to friend OTHER children. Ones that he may not know yet that might be a support, and he needs to know how to keep the friends he has, during the bullying episode.

Friendships include different components at different stages:
Early childhood: In early childhood, your child begins to understand the need for turn taking, but they tend to be egocentric, centered on themselves. Friendship is based on simple play, and friends are the ones who are in the same room with them.

Elementary age Children (Grades 1 to 4): In elementary school, children begin to experience friendships that include give and take. Children begin to associate with others who they see as similar to them in some way, most often in likes and dislikes.

Middle school age children (Grades 5 to 8): In middle school, children are very aware of their effect on their peers and what is said about them. They are also more aware of what they say about others, and the effects it all has. Importance is placed on loyalty, and certain expectations of trust are in place. Friendships are based in common interests and developed through experience sharing. Cliques may form, as children become choosy about their friends. A split between genders is likely to be seen.

High School (Grades 8 to 12): Peer group acceptance is of the ultimate importance. Family is often rejected in favor of peers. Loyalty and trust is expected in friendships. Friendships are formed with people who your child feels understand, recognize them and support them. There is increased understanding that different types of friendships can be experienced.

Friendship skills include:

- being able to introduce oneself to a group.

- starting and maintaining conversations.

- being able ask questions to find out about others.

- awareness and control of tone of voice.

- listening and trying to understand.

- understanding and empathizing with mistakes.

- accepting people for who they are.

- giving and accepting compliments.

- giving and accepting criticism.

- giving and accepting help.

- being cooperative.

- being able to negotiate and problem solve.

- supporting a friend in difficult times.

- supporting a friend in positive growth.

- sharing your space, and your stuff.

- being a good winner and a good loser.

- knowing how to ignore annoyances.

- choosing friends.

When you see your child using these skills, give them positive feedback. Positive feedback breeds more positive behavior.

Activities:

Discuss with your child how they feel when they try to introduce themselves:
•In a group where no one knows each other
•In a group where people know each other, but do not know your child

- In a group where they know the people a little bit but are not good friends

Role play jumping into a conversation and/or introducing themselves with your child. Practice welcoming another child into a conversation by turning your body towards them and widening the talking space circle.

If your child is experiencing bully actions, talk about the friends they have. Are they good friends? Are there opportunities to make new, different friends, or to expand on friendships that are already slightly developed?

Brainstorm ways to meet/introduce yourselves to different people. Use the introduction situations above to develop role plays.

To enhance listening skills, make a habit of reading with your child. Every two or three pages, ask your child to summarize what happened. If a book is complicated, ask for a summarization more often, or if your child is advanced, ask for a summarization at the end, and ask other questions about what happened. This gives your child experience in listening and rephrasing. Empathizing can also be enhanced by discussion the feelings, or potential feelings of the characters, throughout reading.

Talk about compliments in this way with your child, and use the idea for yourself as well: A compliment is a gift. It's rude to refuse a gift. It is important to accept a compliment with a simple "Thank you." Rather than trying to deny it or immediately returning another compliment. Compliments are gifts that can be given for free.

Learning to accept people as they are can start by helping people. Seek out a soup kitchen or food bank that you can help at, as a family. Help your child see that we need to define people by their inner selves, not their outer trappings. Help them see that every person has an important place in the world.

Brainstorm some arguments that your child has had with friends, and define the two positions (ie: One person wants to go to the movie, one wants to go to the youth center) Work through the situation using a friendship problem solving process. Help your child ask the following questions about the disagreement:

1. Why was my position important to me?
2. Why was the other person's position important to them?
3. Is there an obvious compromise? (Can we do both things?)
4. Is there a possible trade off? (We do what you want tonight, and what I want next time.)

Talk openly about jealousy. Are there ever times when you or your child feel jealous of the other person in a friendship? Jealousy tends to be related to one's own self concept. Discussing jealousy can bring into focus the needs a child has in terms of self-concept development. If your daughter is jealous of a friend because the friend is thinner, it points out a body self-concept issue that needs focus. REMEMBER, changing self concept is not about finding and changing the perceived negatives. It is about finding and enhancing the real positives.

To practice ignoring annoyances, practice ignoring annoyances! When you, or your child is annoyed by someone's behavior, ask yourselves "How much will this matter in six months?" (or even tomorrow). For minor annoyances, the answer is not at all. This helps you and your child to think about it in a balanced way. When a behavior cannot be ignored, teach your child distraction. For example, when their sibling is tapping their pen against the table, a child can get up and go to a different room for a different activity without bothering to make a comment.

Have your child keep a friendship diary. They can keep track of whenever they use a friendship skill.

Brainstorm a list of important qualities they want their friends to have, and compare their good friends with the list. Do their good friends have those qualities? Brainstorm a list of qualities that would make them choose not to have someone for a friend.

Protection Nine: Bill of Rights and Responsibilities

The Bill of Rights and Responsibilities is the basis for assertive behavior. Learning and living the ideas in it will prevent both bully actions and victim responses. To print copies of the bill for your bulletin boards or refrigerator, go to http://nosuchthingasabully.com .

Bill of Rights and Responsibilities

1. You have the right to be treated with respect. You have the responsibility to ask for respect, to respect others in return, and to respect yourself.

2. You have the right to have and express your own opinions and feelings. You have the responsibility to do that respectfully and to take responsibility for owning your feelings and opinions.

3. You have the right to be listened to and taken seriously. You have the responsibility to express yourself clearly, simply and calmly and to take yourself seriously on serious matters.

4. You have the right to set your own priorities. You have the responsibility to take the time and effort to follow through.

5. You have the right to say "No" without feeling guilty or making excuses. You have the responsibility to say "No" honestly and directly.

6. You have the right to ask for what you want knowing that others have the same right to say "No".

7. You have the right to ask for information from any source. You have the responsibility to decide if the information is helpful and whether to make use of it.

8. You have the right to make mistakes. You have the responsibility to accept that you don't have to be perfect and the responsibility to learn from your mistakes.

9. You have the right to change your mind. You have the responsibility to accept the consequence of doing so.

10. You have the right to not know all the answers. You have the responsibility to accept that you don't have to know everything and can research the answer, if you wish.

11. You have the right to tell someone you want to take time to think things over. You have the responsibility of doing so and getting back to the other party with your clear answer.

12. You have the right to choose not to assert yourself. You have the responsibility to accept the effects of not asserting yourself and feel okay about it.

Activities:

Be sure to have a discussion about times when your child can't say no, such as when facing a vaccination at the doctor's office or when there is homework to be done. It's important that children know that they can say no at times; and they also must know when they can't.

Depending on the age of your child, you may wish to discuss how not living according to the rights and responsibilities can result in criminal activity. For example, when you engage in stealing you are not respecting the rights of others. You are not respecting others' property. You are not respecting yourself and your positive abilities.

Especially for younger children, ask your child if there are any words in the rights and responsibilities that are difficult to understand.

Discuss some or all of the following questions with your child. Don't worry about having the 'right' answers. The importance of this exercise is in the discussion. Simply talk about different situations and ideas with your child.

How do we know if we are respecting ourselves and others? What kinds of behaviors do we see?

What kinds of ideas and emotions are hard to express?

What are some ways that we can express ourselves clearly?

When have you said no?

What kinds of things might others say no to you about?

When might you not want to answer yes or no right away?

What are some examples of times when you must get information from other people?

What are some examples of learning from mistakes?

What are times where you have or where you might change your mind? What might be some of the consequences of changing your mind?

What kinds of things don't you know the answers to? Discuss the phrase, "You don't know what you don't know." - Anonymous

What are some times where you might decide not to act assertively? (This can be a tough one, so some examples are: When you have to do something anyway, like homework; when it is best to walk away from a situation and think about what you are going to do about it.)

Draw with your child, a picture of a time they made a mistake and discuss what was learned.

We can learn something really well by teaching. Encourage your child teach the rights and responsibilities to another adult who is important in their lives.

Protection Ten: Bully Actions and Victim Responses

At this point, you've done a lot of learning about communicating and have a lot of things to teach your child. Now we're into the meat and potatoes of the issue.

By now, you also know, that this is a whole new approach to the idea of the bullying issue. Whether your child is using bully actions, or victim responses, they are first and foremost – YOUR CHILD. A CHILD. Not a victim, and not a bully, but rather, a child who is using bully actions. Or a child who is using victim responses.

The definition of bullying that is used in this program is as follows:

Bullying = bully actor perspective + action + victim responder perspective where	
bully actor perspective =	desire to hurt + superior power/enjoyment + desire for control/contempt
action =	hurtful + repeated
victim responder perspective =	vulnerability + sense of oppression/unjust treatment

Here is a simpler view for younger children:

You are using a bully action if you

1. want to hurt someone.
2. do something that hurts them.
3. are stronger than them in some way.
4. hurt them more than once.
5. use your extra power to hurt them.
6. enjoy hurting people, and think you are better than them.
7. The people you hurt feel sad, bad and helpless.

You are experiencing bully actions if:

1. someone wants to hurt you
2. someone does something that hurts you.
3. the person is stronger than you in some way.
4. the person hurts you more than once.
5. the person uses her extra power to hurt you.
6. the person enjoys hurting you
7. you feel hurt, sad, bad and helpless.

It may be important to understand the bully prevention strategies that are used in your child's school. Don't be afraid to get involved! A school's number one complaint about bully prevention programs is not having the manpower to implement and maintain a full program. Parents need to get involved in order to create a culture of involvement. Involvement is also a part of teaching your child to "do good, be good and will good"[10]. Become involved in the school with a positive mind set and the intention to help create a safe happy setting for all children. This doesn't need to be about protecting your

---

[10] Barbara Coloroso, The Bully, The Bullied and The Bystander, 2004.

child or "keeping an eye on the bully".

Breaking the definition down into parts makes it easier to understand. Be sure your child understands the definition and understand how the definition is used to evaluate behavior and decide if it is bullying behavior.

Depending on the age of your child, you may also have to address sexual bullying and sexual assault. You also need to be aware of sexual identity bullying. Most often sexual identity bullying comes from home. Has your child ever heard you say "That's so gay." Or "limp-wristed", or "fairy", "butch". Evaluate carefully, because a lot of people DO make comments like this from time to time. Children WILL notice and mirror this.

Remind yourself and your child that you may not even know who in their lives is, or is not gay or lesbian. They may be making comments about a classmate's sexuality, and find out years later that their own brother is gay or their wife's sister is a lesbian.

Sexual identity is an easy bully action tool to use because people tend to feel uncomfortable addressing it. Identify it and don't make talking about it embarrassing. The less secretively sexual identity issues are treated, the less bully action power the issues have.

Make sure your child knows that there are many kinds of bullying, and explain them all. The types of bullying include physical, verbal, emotional, sexual, sexual identity, and cyber bullying, through phone and internet.

Your child needs to be aware that he has a big negative effect on people when he uses bully actions. Discuss the following effects:

- fear of being in parts of the school where bully actions take place. (This might even be the bathroom, imagine being afraid to go to the bathroom!)
- lower grades, poor attendance, less concentration
- difficulty making or keeping friends, sometimes due to the pressure of the bully on other people as well.

Let your child know that students who are bullied are frightened and need friends. Help him understand that it is good to befriend someone who is bullied but also that they may need adult help with the situation.

Explain to him that when someone is using bully actions, it is because they are trying to feel strong and powerful. The person using bully actions can ONLY look strong and powerful if the person they are using bully actions against gets upset. They continue to use bully actions on those who look timid or frightened, those who give them an "entertaining" reaction. (Entertaining reactions tend to be based in the Fight or Flight Response.) Help your child to understand that they can best combat bully actions by becoming confident and believing in themselves – knowing who they are in their own self-concept and not accepting other people's negative labeling. Help your child to understand that learning how to be assertive can protect them from bully actions. There is no better self esteem builder than having control over your life.

Let your child know that ignoring bully actions can be effective, although it may not work the first time it is tried. Teach the students not to give up on this idea. The following are important points for you and your child to know.

When you are using bullying actions, you need to:

1. Learn about feelings, especially anger and sadness. Feeling angry or sad can make you want to treat others badly.

2. Learn about positive ways to handle your feelings, and make sure that you have an adult that you can talk to about your feelings.

3. Learn how to talk in a respectful way.

4. Learn ways to get what you want and need that are respectful.

5. Tell your parents or another adult that you need some help if something has changed in your life and it is making you angry, sad or mad. This might be a new baby, someone dying, your parents divorcing, or anything else that bothers you.

Bullying actions can go on because:

1. A person who is dealing with bully actions might be scared to stand up to the person using them.

2. A person who is dealing with bully actions might feel like they are all alone and have no one to go to for help.

3. A person who is dealing with bully actions might feel bad about themselves and feel like they deserve to be treated badly.

4. A person who is dealing with bully actions might feel like if they try to do something to stop the bully actions they will only get worse.

5. A person who is dealing with bully actions might hope that if they do what the person wants, the person will start to be their friend.

When you are being bullied:

1. Tell someone! Your parents, your grandparents or your teacher, but make sure you tell someone! You can tell them who was involved and if anyone else saw it happen. If you have seen someone being hurt, tell them what you saw. You can tell them what happened and what you did or said. You can tell them where it happened and how often it happens. If you have any injuries, scrapes or bruises make sure you show them to an adult.

2. Be a friend to someone else who is being hurt. Most often people using bully actions don't want to pick on kids who are in groups.

3. Stay away from people who use bully actions if you can. Try ignoring them and walking away. They can't use the bully action on you unless you are there. If it is happening online, go offline completely for several weeks.

4. Stay where teachers or adults can see you. If they can see you being hurt, they will be able to help you, especially if you have made them aware of the bully actions.

5. Don't bring expensive things or lots of money to school.

6. Be confident. People using bully actions like to pick on kids who seem scared. Hold your head up and stand up straight.

7. Don't fight back. Think up things to say ahead of time. Use "I" statements. (Lesson 12) Don't say things that are mean. Deal with the bully action without using a bully action yourself!

8. Don't let the person make you mad or make you react. That is what the person using a bully action wants. Stay calm, ignore, walk away and tell someone.

9. Walk to school with someone.

10. Avoid kids who don't seem to like you or who are mean to you. Stay away from the places where they are, if you can.

11. Say something funny to show that you are not scared.

If you see someone dealing with bully actions:

1. Be friends with that person.

2. Help the person tell an adult.

3. Don't join in when you see bully actions happening.

4. Stand up for someone else, but don't try to fight the person using bully actions yourself. Tell an adult or help your friend tell an adult.

Activities:

Read through the information in the lesson with your child and discuss.

Discuss the following questions with your child:

What types of bully actions do you see or experience?

Name some types of bully actions that you know about. Give some examples.

What victim responses encourage bully actions?

Why do people use bully actions?

Can one person use both bully actions and victim responses?

With your child, come up with responses to bullying that are:
• Ways to ignore bully actions
• Make it clear to the bully that this isn't really important to you.

Discuss what each of you can do to prevent and stop bullying.

Use the following scenarios to discuss bullying situations with your child.

Jerry keeps on following Julia around the school. He teases her about her long legs. Sometimes he tries to corner her alone and scares her. He has even kissed her. Julia is scared of him. A few of her friends know that he is doing this, but she is afraid to tell anyone else. She is worried about him getting really mad at her. No adults seem to be noticing that this is happening. Julia has stopped going to the cafeteria. She has started staying in her classroom for lunch so she doesn't take the chance of running into him.

Are these bullying actions? How do you know?

What can Julia do?

What can her friends do?

How do you think Julia might feel?

How do you think the person using the bully action might feel?

What might happen to Jerry, if Julia and her friends get help?

What might happen to Julia if she doesn't get help?

A new girl, Sylvia, has just arrived at school. She is in a minority culture at school. Much of what she is experiencing is new to her. The most popular group in school decide that she is a loser and that no one should be friends with her. The first month of school is terrible for Sylvia. She has to deal with being called names and being pushed. Her books have even been wrecked. After about a month, she met two girls in the library. Since then they have become friends and the others leave her alone a bit more.

Are these bullying actions? How do you know?

What can Sylvia do?

How might this affect Sylvia?

How could the other students have stopped the bully actions?

Why might the group be using bully actions?

Why have they eased up on their treatment of her?

Benny is worried about going to school. An older kid, James is always punching his shoulders and pinching his

arms and chest. James laughs when he does it. Benny has a whole bunch of bruises. James is bigger than him and Benny just tries to laugh it off and pretend it doesn't hurt, but he is getting worried about going to school.

Are these bully actions? How do you know?

What can Benny do?

How do you think Benny might feel?

How do you think James might feel?

What could bystanders do?

What might happen to James if Benny gets help?

What might happen to James if Benny doesn't get help?

What might happen to Benny if he doesn't get help?

Discuss bully actions and "bullies" found in modern media. This could be any characters that use aggressive behavior to get their own way. Discuss how we make these media characters into heroes and people to admire. Reality television shows can be included in this discussion as well. For ideas about this, go to http://nosuchthingasabully.com

Protection Eleven: Saying No

Saying no is hard! It is one of the things that most of us find uncomfortable at one time or another. Sometimes it's just easier to say yes, to avoid the consequences. Have you ever said yes to your child in order to avoid the consequences of saying no? Most people have.

Part of standing up for yourself in the face of bully actions *is* learning to say no. Learning to say no to being treated badly, learning to say no to accepting the way other people are defining you, learning to say no to going along with bullying by others.

You need to know how to say no, in order for your child to learn how to say no. You need to respect yourself enough to say no when necessary. It might be no to overloading your schedule, or no to how someone treats you. Your child needs to see you controlling your own life, in order to learn that there are ways for them to control their own lives.

A key to saying no is the way the no is given. Often in the process of saying no, the other guy is hurt. You might give the no too quickly, without tact, or you might impose a guilt feeling on them for asking. You might explain too much or too little, or you might passively aggressively say no – by putting the other guy off and not really giving him a clear answer in the end. People become angry because of their feelings, not because of the no. The trick is to learn how to say no respectfully, clearly and at the right times for you.

Here are some ideas for changing your perceptions about saying no:

- It is your right to meet your needs by saying no. It is your responsibility to say no in a way that is timely and respectful.
- When you say no to one thing, you are making room for yourself to be able to say yes to something else that is important to you.
- Saying yes when you really want to say no will cause you to be resentful and angry about the request. Saying yes when you really mean no can ruin relationships.
- If you have been doing your share to keep a relationship going, and you are unable at this time to grant a favor to the other person, a clear explanation rather than avoidance or trickery is necessary.
- Have an open and honest look at your life as it is at present. Are you spending time on the things that you value the most? Is much of your time taken up with things that you don't value? Arrange your time so that the majority of your time is spent doing things that match your important values, the parts of your life that you feel are important.

Some solid ideas for helping yourself to say no follow.

- When you say no to one request, look for something else that you can say yes about. If your child can have a treat later, tell them what time they can have it, instead of simply saying 'no'. If someone asks you to chair a meeting that you will be attending, decline respectfully and make an offer that you are willing to follow through on, such as bringing refreshments.

- Don't answer right away; give yourself time to think about it. Phrases such as "I will check my schedule and get back to you," or "I need some time to think about that," are helpful. Get back to the person in a timely manner. You can even give the other person an idea of when you will be able to answer. "I can let you know next week." Then do it!

- Be clear when you say no. Don't use words such as "maybe" or "probably" when what you really mean is no. It is respectful to others to let them know where you stand. You can be clearer in saying no by being aware of your body language. Shake your head "no" and look the other person in the eye.

- Make a point of saying no to something every day, just for practice. Try it out on some telemarketers!

- If you must say no to someone who you would like to try to help, express that you would like to be able to help. "I can't do that tonight. I wish I could help. Please ask me another time."

- Express empathy to the person asking, so they feel understood. "I can understand why you need help with that. I bet it's a big job."

- Start off by saying no. It is easier to back up what you've already said than it is to try to get back to saying no after you've said a few sentences.

- Flip flopping your answer often can be confusing and difficult for people.

Go through the following ideas with your child at their level.

Remember the Bill of Rights and Responsibilities. "You have the right to say no. You have the responsibility to say no clearly and respectfully."

When you have to say no to one thing, you might be able to say yes to something else. "No, I can't come over today. How about tomorrow?"

If you must say no, and you would still like to help, look for other ideas. "No you can't copy my homework. I'll help you with yours if you want."

Say no and give a reason. "No, I don't like amusement park rides."

Be clear when you want to say no. Don't say maybe or probably if you mean no. "No. I don't want to do that."

Say no, and add thank you. "No thank you."

Change the subject. "Let's break this window."
"No, let's go to my place and play video games."

Keep on saying no.
"Let's cut up these books."
"No, that is wrong to do."
"C'mon, Let's do it!"
"No, that is wrong to do."
"It will be fun!"
"No, that is wrong to do."

Use your smarts to stay away from trouble. If you know of places where there could be trouble stay away.

Say no to bullying right when it starts by saying "It is not okay for you to treat me that way." As a bystander say no to bullying by paying attention to how others are being treated. Stand up and say, "NO. It is not okay to treat him/her that way!"

Use your body language to help you say no.
"Let's hit that new kid!"
"No." and walk away

Activities:

Practice saying no with your child. Stand in front of the mirror, stand up straight and say "NO". You can also use this time to talk about saying No to stranger danger and yelling really loud.

Start noticing how much you say "no" in a day, and how you say it. Talk about it during the day with your child.

Talk with your child about times when you both have to say yes.

Talk with your child about times when you both have to say no.

When you are watching television commercials, practice saying no to them.

Protection Twelve: "I" Sentences

In order to teach "I" sentences to your child, you have to have a good understanding of them as well.

Using "I" sentences can help to clarify thoughts and express your desire to deal with conflict in a positive manner. An "I" sentence is made of three parts.

1.   "I feel _____ ."

Starting off with your emotions about the situation puts the focus on the speaker. A sentence that begins with "You…" will most often be seen by the other guy as blaming, or accusing. Starting off a conversation by blaming someone puts up walls that makes further positive discussion difficult. Starting off with emotion tells the other guy that there are true effects of the situation that must be resolved.

> "I feel angry."
> "I feel anxious."
> "I feel stressed."

2.   "When …   "
        "About the …"
        "About my … "

The second part of an "I" sentence involves naming the action that distresses you. Be concrete and specific. Don't put in any assumptions. This must be facts, and must be non-blaming and non-judgmental.

> "I feel angry when your tone of voice sounds angry to me."
> "I feel anxious when you stay out really late."
> "I feel stressed about my workload."

3. "Could we try…?"
    "I'd like to talk about it with you and see what we come up with."
    "What if we…"
    "I'd like to try…"

The third part of an "I" statement looks toward the future and suggests options for resolution. This will take many forms, but again works best if it remains non-blaming and non-judgmental. Who wants to work towards a solution when they feel judged and blamed?!

To put it all together then:

> "I feel angry when your tone of voice sounds angry to me. I would appreciate talking in a calm way."

> "I feel anxious about the report getting done on time. I'd like to discuss ways that we can be sure the work gets done."

> "I feel stressed about my workload. I'd like to talk about it with you and see what we come up with."

Plan ahead. In the beginning, using "I" sentences will feel awkward and new. It will be necessary to work at the phrasing and to think about what you are going to say. If all you can come up with is: "I feel angry when you breathe, could you please stop," you must work harder at identifying the specific issues!

Being assertive means choosing how to react; not just reacting. Taking the time to decide what you will say is choosing how you will react. These examples of "I" sentences show ways you can start off a difficult conversation. "I" sentences can also be used throughout a conversation in order to clearly express your feelings and wishes.

The following gives you other language to explain "I" sentences to your child:

1. An "I" sentence starts with "I" because then the focus is on you. They use feelings, because it's pretty hard to argue with feelings. If you say you are sad or angry, then no one can really argue with that. How you feel is how you feel.

> I feel sad
> I feel sorry

2. The middle part of an "I" sentence tells what is happening.

> I feel sad when I am hit.
> I feel sorry that I hit you.

3. The next sentence has answers to the problem.

> I feel sad when I am hit. Please don't hit me again.
> I feel sorry that I hit you. I won't hit you anymore.

A bystander can also use an "I sentence", for example, stating "I am upset when I see people being mistreated. I need you to stop that." Parents can also use "I" sentences with their children. "I" sentences enhance relationships and understanding.

Activities:

Use the following scenarios to practice making "I" statements.

There is a girl that you only see in the hallways who comments on your clothes each day at school. You don't appreciate her commentaries. Use an "I" sentence to tell her how you feel and what you want her to do.
(You are a bystander, how can you use an "I" sentence to intervene?)

A friend is pressuring you to have a cigarette and you don't want to. How can you say no, using an "I" sentence?
(You are a bystander, how can you use an "I" sentence to intervene?)

You are standing in line at a drinking fountain and someone pushes ahead of you. What will you say? Use an "I" sentence. (You are a bystander, how can you use an "I" sentence to intervene?)

You are eating in the cafeteria and another student comes in, threatens you and takes your lunch. Use an "I" sentence to the student. (You are a bystander, how can you use an "I" sentence to intervene?)

Your friend keeps on wanting to borrow money from you. He has asked again and you can't lend him any more money until he has paid you what he owes you. Use an "I" sentence to tell him so.

Your household chore is taking out the garbage and cleaning the bathroom. You hate these jobs. You would rather sweep the floor and vacuum the rugs. Use an "I" sentence to tell your mom or dad.

Notice that these are not all bullying situations – an "I" sentence is handy a lot of the time.

Use the scenarios above one at a time, and answer the following questions.

How would you handle it if you are assertive?
How would you handle it if you are aggressive?
How would you handle it if you are passive?
How would you handle it if you are passive-aggressive?

Use "I" sentences in every day life, and notice out loud when you and your child are using them.

Protection Thirteen: Always and Never

   This is a short, self explanatory lesson. When you use the words always and never, you escalate conflict and are generally communicating poorly. If you tell your child they never take the garbage out, they can think of the one time they did, and you are automatically wrong. Things are very rarely always or never, however when in conflict we often think that they are. We believe we are never treated fairly, or that we always have to do more. Thinking "always" or "never" makes your emotional reactions stronger, and also can give the other guy a stronger fight or flight reaction.
   Sometimes people don't think they need to listen when they hear another person talking in extremes. It is better to put forward your case with facts.

Activities:

Talk with your child about the times your child and you use the words always and never.

Look for truths that really ARE always or never. For example...A lit match that is held to dry paper will always start a fire. Evaluate if your "truths" really are the truth, or if they need more detail.

During everyday living, watch for the use of the words always and never in your home.

Use the following paragraph and discuss what you need more information about to know if the use of always and never (and every time) is true. How can this be said in a way that would be more accurate?

"Jeff always hits me on the playground. Every time I go to the swings he pushes me down and tells me that I can't use them. He never listens to me, and he always teases me."

"You never do what I ask you to do."

"You always call me names."

"You never clean up after yourself."

Protection Fourteen: Questions

Knowing good ways to ask questions facilitates friendships, introduction to groups and increases problem solving abilities. It's an important friendship skill, and of course, strong friendships are an important barrier to experiencing bully actions.

The difference between open and closed questions can be somewhat abstract, and it can be difficult to tell the difference. Questions can even be defensive...How about when your child yells "Why do you hate me?"

Explain why this is important (as above) and review these ways of asking questions with your child:

Different kinds of questions can be confusing but it is important to be able to tell the difference. There are closed questions and open questions. A closed question only asks for a little bit of information. They can be answered with a yes or a no, or sometimes by giving the little bit of information that is being asked about. Open questions require more information to answer. They can help you to understand what the other person has said. Knowing how to ask open questions is an important part of getting to know someone else.

Some examples of closed questions:
Are you all right? (yes or no)
Is this the right way to do this? (yes or no)
What is your address? (62 Bay Street)
Where do you go to school? (Brighton School)

Some examples of open questions:
What do you think?
What interests you?
What do you do for fun?
Why is math your favorite subject in school?

Another type of question is "defensive questions". Defensive questions are often said with negative "tone" – "What are you doing here?" "Why are you doing that?" "Didn't you do that yet?" Questions can change depending on how they are said. A question can sound nasty. Think about how a mom might say "Why aren't you home yet?" if a child was supposed to be home half an hour ago.

Activities:

Try to play a game where you have a conversation with your child using only questions back and forth. No answers!

Brainstorm a list of questions together. Discuss each question. What are possible answers? Is it an open or closed question? Reinforce that it is often hard to tell!

Ask your child a question, have him answer it, and then ask you a question. You answer it and ask another question, and so on, for as long as you choose.

Protection Fifteen: Tone of Voice

Have you ever had a conversation with your child that went like this?

You: Did you do your chores?

Child: No (said with negative or angry tone).

You: Please don't use that tone of voice with me.

Child: I don't know what you are talking about.

Your child may or may not be aware of the tone of his or her voice. To give your child the benefit of the doubt, make her aware of the way tone can change the meanings of words.

Talk to your child from the point of view that we all have different tones of voice to use and that it is a perfectly natural thing. It is also a very positive thing to have control over when, where and how we use our tone. Tone is not only negative, although we tend to think of it that way. It is important for both you and your children to be sure that your tone reflects whatever it is that you intend to say. We've all been in a situation where what we say comes out more angrily than intended – or distorted in some way.

In terms of preventing bully actions, being aware of tone and able to control it assists in two ways. Awareness of tone is a friendship skill, and can facilitate positive friendships growth, which prevents bullying. Control of tone is also a friendship skill, and can assist with standing up for someone who is experiencing bully actions. Knowing how to sound firm can help put off a person using bully actions.

Activities:

"I didn't hit her."
Guide your child in an exercise where a stronger accent is placed on each indicated word. Both of you say the following sentences, with a stronger accent on the bold word.

I didn't hit her.
I *didn't* hit her.
I didn't *hit* her.
I didn't hit *her*.

Four statements; four distinct meanings. Discuss what each different sentence means. This is a quick way to show your child (and yourself!) that how words are said can change the meaning of a sentence.

Talk about the words that get thrown around when someone uses negative tone. These might include lippy, smart alec, smarty pants, "Don't use that tone with me." Let them know that using negative tone is not the most effective way to get what they want. Discuss when tone has worked to get them what they wanted and when it has not worked. What kind of tones work? Which don't?

Talk with your child about:
What do you already know about tone of voice?
Does it sometimes work for you to have a rude tone of voice? Do you get what you want?
Why does it work? When does it not work?
Why doesn't it work?
What is a worst case scenario for you about using a negative tone?

Are there situations where you are more likely to have negative or positive tone in your voice?

Are there times when it seems like a good idea to have negative or positive tone in your voice?

Brainstorm some other types of tone? (For example, excited or kind).

Protection Sixteen: Body Language

If a child looks confident, and appears as though they can take care of themselves, they will be less likely to be bullied. Both you and your children must be aware of what body language is saying. Body language is amazing.

You show people a lot of emotions that you don't intend to show them, whether you are aware of it or not. Sometimes you are angry and don't even know how angry you look or how angry your body language is. Other times you might be sad and not even know how sad your body language is. You might look vulnerable. Think about it,

When you are tired you might:
- Rub your eyes
- Put your head in your hands
- Close your eyes
- Yawn
- Stretch

When you are excited you might
- Be shaky
- Be very active
- Hold your stomach
- Be jittery

When you are angry you might:
- Put your hands across your chest
- Frown, in your mouth and your forehead
- Shake your fist or stomp your foot

People use your body language to make opinions about you. Someone using bully actions who sees you walking with slumped shoulders and looking at the ground, might think you are a good target. If you look angry, people might be afraid to approach you.

Another part of body language is understanding body space. Intimate: 0 - 18 inches, Personal 1.5 - 4 feet, Social 4 - 10 feet, Public: 10 feet and beyond

Understanding body space allows your child to use spacing between himself and others appropriately, particularly if a child appears very shy or very aggressive.

Activities:

Here is a body space exercise :

- Stand 18 inches apart and throw a ball. This is intimate space. Discuss when this it is appropriate to be this close to someone.
- Stand 4 feet apart and throw a ball. This is personal space. Personal space is regular talking space. Discuss when it is appropriate to use this spacing.
- Stand about 7 feet apart and throw a ball. This is social space. Social space is where you might stand if you have just met someone. Discuss when you might use this amount of space.
- Stand 12 feet apart and throw a ball. This is public space. This is how much room you can give someone if you don't know them at all.

Discuss what kind of spacing (generally public) is appropriate if someone is using bully actions against your child?

Have your child use the body language that goes with the descriptions above.

Have your child practice standing up straight and looking confident. Stand in front of the mirror with them, and practice yourself.

Stand in front of each other and BE the mirror for your child. Have your child act out different body language types, and copy them, as though you are the mirror.

Talk about music and body language. What kind of body language is in music videos?

Watch some television shows together and talk about body language that you see.

For younger children, make up an action poem to recite. Simply brainstorm different actions – Hand on hips, arms across chest, arms out for a hug. String them together and say them, doing the action at the same time.

Have a box ready with the names of some emotions. Use the body language that goes with the emotion to play charades, taking turns with your child. For a list of emotion words, go to http://nosuchthingasabully.com .

Protection Seventeen: Thinking

How we perceive our daily situations is often inaccurate and can make conflicts worse. When you are not thinking clearly, you can become more emotional. You feel more defensive and conflict escalates. The more extreme your thinking is, the more extreme your fight or flight reaction will be as well. You can choose whether your thinking, and thus your reaction, will be positive or negative.

We actually have a choice about how we are going to think. The exact same thing can happen to two different people, and they will react to it differently depending on their thinking.

Imagine that two boys, at the same time, are asked to babysit. One boy thinks "Babysitting! That's for girls! I can't believe they asked me to babysit!" The other boy thinks "Babysitting! I haven't tried that before. It will be a good chance to try something and make some money." The first boy might spend some time being angry about how he was asked to babysit. He may not realize that times have changed and that boys care for children just as much as girls now. The second boy will have positive feelings. He will feel productive and able.

Different thoughts = different feelings = different actions.

Activities:

Brainstorm situations where someone could react in a positive or negative way, depending on their thinking.

How can your thinking cause you to use a bully action?

How can your thinking cause you to use a victim response?

How can your thinking keep you from stepping up to help someone else who is being bullied?

Write down some of the thoughts you have when you see someone being bullied.

Write down some of the thoughts you have when you have used a bully action.

Protection Eighteen: Inaccurate Thinking

Everyone thinks inaccurately at times. The first step to balanced thinking is gaining an understanding of how your thinking is inaccurate.

We all do it. Inaccurate thinking is unbalanced thinking. Not mentally ill unbalanced, just an every day, normal kind of unbalanced.

Inaccurate thinking is the kind of thinking that allows you to make assumptions about people: "Bill is just bad, all bad." It allows you to perceive situations as traumas: "This is the worst thing that could have happened." It allows you to feel that you have no control and that the currents of life just carry you wherever they choose. Or that you can control others. Everyone experiences different levels and combinations of inaccurate thinking.

Inaccurate thinking doesn't take all the facts into consideration. It focuses on extremes – usually the extreme negative.

Inaccurate thinking is a habit that is developed over a period of years. If you really think about it, you probably learned your inaccurate thinking from a close role model. Does your mother tell you what you "should do," or "should have done"? Does your father talk about how politicians always lie and pastors never do? Types of thinking are modeled for us. You pick up your own style of thinking along the way, based on your experiences and beliefs. You may believe stereotypes that make it easier to make assumptions about people. Assumptions about people will block communication and likely lead to conflict. You may have had experiences that lead you to believe that a certain type of person (male or female, Aboriginal or Caucasian, etc.) can't be trusted. Beliefs are the result of your experiences. Once you have a certain belief you tend to see the things that support that belief and ignore the things that don't. Changing beliefs is possible, not easy, but possible. The reason that inaccurate thinking affects people so severely is because how you think about a situation will determine how you feel about it. You have emotions based on your thoughts. Some of your thoughts are noticed, some of them are not, and you react emotionally to most of them.

If you experience a great deal of inaccurate thinking, relationships may be affected. Knowing that your thoughts are inaccurate helps you to balance your thinking, which you will learn more about in the next lesson.

Some kinds of inaccurate thinking, and their associations to bullying:

Too much control or not enough control: You can only control your own reactions. You do not control other people.

(If you are experiencing bully actions, you may feel you have no control, which will lead to more helplessness. Knowing that you can control your own reactions can give you control over some of your situation. If you are using bully actions, you may feel you have some right to control other people. You don't. If you are a bystander you may think you have no control of the situation, but you do control how you respond.)

Make me Happy: Others can not make us happy. You must make yourself happy with your own thinking and your own attitudes.

(If you are experiencing bully actions, you may think they have to stop before you can be happy. This is false, you

can still find happiness within yourself and the things you like to do. If you are using bully actions, you may escalate your use of them if people aren't making you happy. Remember that YOU are responsible for your own choices and happiness.)

Overthinking Danger: Planning and dwelling on dangerous situations won't keep them from happening. Make your safety plan and then put it out of your head.

(If you are experiencing bully actions, it is common to think about the danger a lot, and to feel anxious. Making a plan and following it can prevent this anxiety.)

Avoiding: Avoiding things that are making you anxious will only make you more anxious. You must face up to them.

(If you are experiencing bully actions, tell someone and get some help in facing the problem!)

Comparisons: There is no sense comparing yourself to others. There will always be someone who measures up better or worse against you.

(If you are using bully actions, you might compare yourself to others and lash out against those who you think are better or worse than you in some way.)

Anger is just Anger: Anger has an underlying emotion that sometimes feels "weaker". It might be sadness, or fear, but there is usually something under the anger.

(If you are using bully actions or victim responses, you must understand and deal with the emotions that are underneath anger that you have.)

Black and White Thinking: You, other people, or situations are all bad or all good.

(If you are experiencing bully actions, you might look at other people and think they are only bad. If you are using bully actions, you might think the same thing. You need to know that everyone has good parts and bad parts to them. You have to get to know them to find out more about them.)

Negative Focus: Getting caught up in noticing only negative things about yourself, other people or situations.

(If you are experiencing bully actions, you might believe a lot of negative things about yourself or others. If you are using bully actions, you might focus on the negatives in others to justify your own behavior.)

Overgeneralizing: Watch thinking that uses the words always, never and every time.

(If you are experiencing bully actions, you have to be able to explain accurately what is happening so that people can understand.)

Melodramatic Thinking: Everything is a catastrophe!

(Again, you have to be accurate in your thoughts and explanations about what you are experiencing. Very few things are true catastrophes!)

Assumptions: You may assume things are true without having the facts.

(When you are experiencing bully actions you may begin to believe and associate things with it that are not true.

These might be assumptions, and they could make the problem worse.)

Mistakes mean that I am bad and don't know what I am doing: Mistakes are meant to be made and are meant to be learned from.

(If you have used bully actions, you can understand that you've made mistakes, and can learn from them.)

Everyone must like me: It's not possible for everyone to like everyone else.

(If you are experiencing bully actions, remember that you don't have to keep friends that hurt you. Everyone is not going to like everyone else, even though we might still have to be in fairly close contact, as in school.)

Should: The word should is usually used to make ourselves or other people feel guilty.

(If you are experiencing bully actions, you might start to believe the hurtful things that are being said about you and thinking "I should be...",thinner, smarter, or whatever. Should is an unhelpful word to use for yourself or others.)

In case your child is younger, these simpler definitions are also provided for your use. The applications to bullying seen above apply. It is not important that you and your child understand ALL of these. It is important that you become able to pick out the types that you are using.

All good or all bad: We all have parts of us that are good and parts of us that are bad. Maybe you are a really good friend who gets a bit bossy sometimes. Or maybe your friend is usually kind, except when you want to share a certain thing that she has. No one is all good or all bad. We all have good and bad parts of us.

Anger is just anger: When we feel angry, we are usually feeling something else too. The something else is usually something like scared or hurt or sad.

The people around me must make me happy: Sometimes we feel like if everyone around us would give us what we want, we would be happy. Happiness doesn't come from getting everything that you want. You can have all the latest toys and computer games and still not be happy. Happiness comes from inside and from the way you think about your life.

Mistakes are bad: Sometimes when we make a mistake, we feel like what we did was bad and we are bad. You are not bad because you make mistakes! Making mistakes happens because we are people. All people make mistakes. We can learn from our mistakes.

Activities:

Use the examples tor eview the types of inaccurate thinking, and also brainstorming other examples.

Black and White	I hate you, mom! Steve is just all bad! I'm a total idiot!
Overgeneralizing	You never let me do anything! I have to do all the work in the house!

Melodramatic	This is the worst thing that could have happened!
Assumptions	I've never seen her go, but I know she's there all the time!
Control	I want you to do what I want to do! There is nothing I can do.
Should	I should be a better person. I should be able to do that.
Make me happy	If everyone would do what they should, I would be happy. I can't do anything that makes me happy.
Nobody likes me	I'm worthless because I'm not popular. I'm not in sports, so I'm a loser.
Mistakes are bad	I can't believe I said that out loud. What a loser! I'll never get this right!
Overthinking danger	I'm always worrying about getting hurt. Those thoughts are constantly in my head.
Comparisons	She's prettier than me. I'm ugly. He's better at sports than me. I'm weak.

Protection Nineteen: Automatic Thoughts

We send ourselves a lot of automatic thoughts each day. This is a phenomenon that occurs for everyone at some level. Your automatic thoughts are often connected to the types of inaccurate thinking you use. For example if you tend to compare yourself to others negatively, your inaccurate thoughts may reflect that. "I'm so fat", "I'm so ugly."

Automatic thoughts take different forms for different people. Some may experience automatic thoughts as sentences flashing through their brain. Others may see pictures of past or anticipated events and situations. Some may experience memories of comments made about them personally. They may hear voices from conversations they have had in the past. Automatic thoughts may be thoughts that you have about yourself, or about what someone thinks of you. They may be thoughts about others, or about the world.

You don't always notice your automatic thoughts. They flash by so quickly that you are frequently consciously unaware of their content. Automatic thoughts are most often negative and they are most often believed. Automatic thoughts will often remain completely unnoticed until you are encouraged to notice and evaluate them.

The examples of automatic thoughts are many and diverse. What they will be for you will depend on what your past experiences have been. They are linked to the forms of inaccurate thinking you use. Some negative automatic thoughts might include:
"I'm such a big loser."
"No one would ever want to be with me."
"I can't do anything right."

"I'm no good at sports."
"I'm fat."
"I'm a bad parent."

Others might include memories of other people making negative comments about you, or examples of times when you feel you have not been successful.

One example of automatic thoughts might be the rerun that happens in your head about a situation you've just experienced. You may find yourself repeating the situation mentally, worrying about it, worrying what people might be saying or thinking about you. Another example of a situation involving automatic thoughts is the woman who feels great about herself in the morning, but by noon has decided that she is a fat slob. As it is unlikely that there was any great weight gain in the four hours from 8:00 am to 12:00 pm, it is likely that she has had automatic thoughts that have led her to an emotional reaction.

This brings us to the reason that automatic thoughts can be so devastating. You react emotionally to your thoughts. If your thoughts about yourself, others and the world are consistently negative, you will experience consistently negative emotions. This affects your self-concept. When your self-concept is negatively affected, you become at risk of accepting and integrating other people's negative opinions about you. In the context of bullying, when a child begins to accept negative opinions about themselves, and integrate those thoughts and beliefs into their being, they are susceptible to turning the anger that is created towards themselves. They come to believe the negatives that others are handing to them.

In order to prove or disprove automatic thoughts, the thought must be caught, noted and examined for evidence. Learning how to do a thought record will help you to do just that, catch the thought, remain aware of the thought, and examine the thought for supporting evidence, or contradicting evidence. The end result is a more balanced way of looking at self, others and the world that takes into consideration both negative and positive aspects.

Explain to your child:

You have to do something with all those automatic thoughts that you have. Learning balanced thinking techniques can help you to feel confident and sure of yourself.

When you believe the negative messages about yourself, it shows. If you believe you are a loser, or if you think you will never do anything right, you will have trouble standing up straight, talking to people, trouble in all sorts of ways. When you believe the negative messages about yourself, it is hard to feel confident. When someone says something negative about you, you might begin to believe it.

It is important to ask yourself the questions in the next lesson, in order to balance out your automatic thoughts.

It can help to write out the answers to your balanced thinking questions. Sometimes, when you have the same thought over and over you can just look at your answers and feel better.

In a straight association to bullying, children taking on the three roles, might have the following automatic thoughts:

A child using bully actions:
They did it first, so it's okay.
He's a loser anyway, he deserves it.
I'm tough.

A child using victim actions:
What did I do to deserve this?
I'm such a loser.
I wish I had more friends.

A child who is a bystander:
There's nothing I can do.
I'm glad that's not me.
I am scared to do anything.

Activities:

Brainstorm automatic thoughts that you and your child use. Talk about how you each feel when you have those thoughts.

Using the following role plays, take some guesses at what kind of automatic thoughts each person is having:

Tammy and Julie used to be good friends but lately Julie is spending more time with Shelley. Tammy is angry and is yelling at Julie about it. Julie is yelling back.

Billy keeps on bumping into Joey and hip checking him into the locker. Billy says it's no big deal and Joey can't take a joke when Joey tries to talk to him about it.

Marnie and Olivia were good friends but Olivia has been going to parties and drinking and Marnie doesn't want to be involved. Marnie and Olivia are both talking about each other in the hallways.

Go on to the next lesson to learn a balanced thinking tool.

Protection Twenty: Balanced Thinking

Balanced thinking provides your child with a tool that contributes to:

- problem-solving
- building positive relationships
- avoiding criminal and other negative activity
- avoiding and recovering from mental illness or anxiety
- managing conflict
- providing a strong basis for adult life.

In order to teach this to your child, you must learn it as well! Here is an example of a situation and a thought record from a parental perspective:

> Sue Ann has been worried about her relationship with her seventeen-year-old daughter, Carissa. Carissa has been pulling away from the family, spending more time with her friends than she does at home. She doesn't tolerate questioning about her activities very well, resulting in a lot of arguments. Last night she didn't come home at all. Sue Ann hasn't approached her about not coming home yet. She fears that it will just lead to a blow out and Carissa will end up leaving. Sue Ann doesn't know if Carissa is using drugs, alcohol, or having sex, but it certainly seems like a possibility. Sue Ann doesn't know if she should push the situation further, or let it go, or just what to do. Sue Ann is feeling very distressed and confused.

Sue Ann's Thought Record

Situation: Thinking about how to approach Carissa about staying out all night.

Emotions: Fear, anxiety

Automatic Thoughts:
She is going to get mad and leave.
I'm going to yell my head off.
This is going to ruin any future relationship between us.

Sue Ann picks the automatic thought that is the most distressing to her. She becomes very upset thinking about the future relationship between herself and her teenage daughter, and how that relationship is going to be affected by all this fighting. She will focus on that automatic thought for the rest of the thought record.

Information that supports the automatic thought:
This is going to ruin any future relationship between us.
Carissa has walked out of the house before.
We have been fighting a lot lately. We say hurtful things to each other.
Carissa is getting older. She has older friends. She might just decide to move out.

Information that does not support the automatic thought: This is going to ruin any future relationship between us.
Carissa has walked out of the house before, but she has always come back.

Even if Carissa were to move out, it would not necessarily mean that our relationship would end.
If I talk to Carissa respectfully and don't say those hurtful things, she responds better.
Teenagers at age 17 tend towards pulling away from their families.
Teenagers must be aware of the house rules and their boundaries.

A more balanced thought:

Although talking to Carissa about staying out all night may be difficult, it does not have to mean that our relationship will end. Carissa may be mad at me, but if I treat her respectfully things will be okay. If and when Carissa does decide to move away from home, it does not have to mean that our relationship will end, just that it will change.

This can be repeated with the other automatic thoughts if they are also attached to strong emotions. This can also be repeated in many different situations. People often have the same repeated automatic messages. Thought reruns. If thought records are written down, they can be re-used. When the thought rerun happens, the already written thought record can serve as a quick reminder of a more balanced way to think about the situation, or the thought.

Using the following questions, you will guide your child through the scenarios and help them think about the automatic thoughts in a balanced way.

Balanced Thinking Questions

1. What is my automatic thought?

2. What is true about the automatic thought?

3. What is not true about the automatic thought?

4. What is a different way to think about it?

Review the automatic thoughts that you previously brainstormed. Brainstorm the reasons balanced thinking is important.

Use the following Balanced Thinking scenarios with your child. Some ideas are written in, but you and you child may have other answers:

- Someone misses an important catch in a baseball game. Automatic thought "I can't do anything right!"
  - What is true about the automatic thought? "I just missed the catch."
  - What is not true about the automatic thought? "There are other things that I do right. I have caught tough hits before. I have good marks in school."
  - What is another way to think about it? "I do lots of things right. This time I missed the catch, that doesn't really mean that I can't do anything right."

- Someone gets a poor mark on a test. Automatic thought "I am stupid!"
  - What is true about the automatic thought? "I just got a bad mark."
  - What is not true about the automatic thought? "I am smart enough to have passed

other tests. I didn't study hard enough for this one."
  - o What is another way to think about it? "I failed the test, but that doesn't mean I'm stupid. I've passed other tests and can learn from my mistake and study harder."

- Someone gets bullied at school. Automatic thought "This is my fault because I'm fat."
  - o What is true about the automatic thought? "I am overweight."
  - o What is not true about the automatic thought? "No one deserves to be treated badly no matter how they look."
  - o What is another way to think about it? "I can control my weight if I work at it. Other people being mean or rude is not my fault.

- Someone sees someone else gets bullied at school. Automatic thought "There is nothing I can do."
  - o What is true about the automatic thought? "It is a hard situation."
  - o What is not true about the automatic thought? "There are things that I can do."
  - o What is another way to think about it? "I am frightened but I can make choices about what I am going to do. I can ask an adult for help.

Use the list of brainstormed automatic thoughts from the previous less and answer the questions using them. Access a thought record form at http://nosuchthingasabully.com

Protection Twenty One: The Anxiety Equation

Feeling anxious and distressed about events taking place in your life can cause a great deal of stress. Adults do not own the right to be anxious. Your child is living in anxious times, and is exposed to a great deal more than you ever were. Talking to your child about anxieties is an important conversation to have.

The Anxiety Equation[11] isn't made of numbers. It looks like this:

$$\text{Anxiety} = \frac{\underline{\text{High Estimation of Danger}}}{\text{Low Estimation of Coping Skills and Resources}}$$

In order to be anxious you must have these elements: a high estimation of danger, and a low estimation of your ability to cope with it.

So what does this mean? It means that when you feel anxious or scared, you will often be thinking that the danger is higher than it is. Think about the worst thing that could happen. Is it as bad as you thought?

Now think about the skills you have to cope with the danger. When you are anxious, you usually think that you are not going to be able to cope! But you have a ton of coping skills. You can use balanced thinking. You can use problem solving. You can use brainstorming. You can ask for help. You can use your good communication skills. You can practice relaxing. You can get any help or information that you need.

---

[11] Greenberger & Padesky, "Mind Over Mood – Change How You Feel By Changing the Way You Think," 1995

Coping skills can be very simple. They could be:
- being able to take time alone.
- being able to talk to friends.
- knowing what is relaxing for you.
- knowing how to brainstorm.

These three questions help you to work through the anxiety equation.

1. What is the worst thing that can happen?
2. Is it as bad as you thought it would be?
3. What must you do to handle it?

Activities:

Use the following examples to work through the anxiety equation.

Issue: Fear of not doing well in a sports event.

(Overestimation of Danger)
Answer the questions to assess **Real Danger:**

Is there a chance that I could be more scared than I need to be?
What facts show that this is something that I do have to worry about?
What facts show that this is something that I don't have to worry about?

(Underestimation of Skills and Resources) **What I must do:**

Be aware of my own abilities.
Know that this is a team sport, and winning isn't just up to me. Talk to the coach if I am unsure about what I am supposed to be doing or need more information.

Issue: Worry that homework will not be complete

(Overestimation of Danger)
Answer the questions to assess **Real Danger:**
Is there a chance that I am more worried than I need to be?
What facts show that this is something that I do have to worry about?
What facts show that this is something that I don't have to worry about?

(Underestimation of Skills and Resources) **What I must do:**

Make a plan for how to get the homework done.
Schedule certain times during the day to do homework.
Have a specific place where I like spending time to do homework.
Ask my parents for help in making a plan.
Ask my teacher if I have questions about the homework.
Ask a friend for help.

Issue: Fear that my friends won't like me if I don't do what they want.

(Overestimation of Danger)
Answer the questions to assess **Real Danger:**

Is there a chance that I am more worried than I need to be?
What facts show that this is something that I do have to worry about?
What facts show that this is something that I don't have to worry about?

(Underestimation of Skills and Resources) **What I must do:**

Practice saying no with my friends.
Know that if my friends are forcing me to do something

that I don't want to do they are not good friends.
Know that even if my friends decide to dump me, I can
make other friends.

**Issue: Fear about walking to school because of
experiencing bully actions.**

(Overestimation of Danger)
Answer the questions to assess **Real Danger**:

Is there a chance that I am more worried than I need to be?
What facts show that this is something that I do have to
worry about?
What facts show that this is something that I don't have to
worry about?

(Underestimation of skills and resources) **What I must do:**

Tell an adult. Be clear about what is happening.
Make a different plan for how to get to school that is still
convenient.
Walk with a group.

Now brainstorm things that you and your child feel anxious
about and work through the anxiety equation with her.

Protection Twenty Two: Taking Care of Yourself

Your child needs to know that taking care of himself is important TO himself. Ultimately it doesn't have anything to do with what he is being told. Taking care of himself is done for his own well being.

This is basically a quick health lesson, added in because in order to be bullyproof, you have to be taking care of yourself. If a child is healthy, physically and emotionally, he is less likely to engage in bully actions or victim responses.

Help your child understand not only what he has to do to take care of himself, but also why, in terms of himself and his own life.

Activities:

For younger children, wash yourself like you would in the shower, washing each part and mirroring each other as you do it.

Have a discussion with your child about personal care. Introduce a nutritional food guide and healthy diets. If you are not already eating according to a healthy food guide, share making the change with your child.

Go to http://nosuchthingasabully.com for extra information regarding sleep health and sleep meditation.

Protection Twenty Three: Lucky or Unlucky

Your child needs to understand life in a holistic way. Children often see adults over-reacting to things that happen in their lives. A quick reaction is often unwarranted and it is truly hard to know right away if something is bad or good. This is important when our children are going through hard times, because there is the desire to end the hard time for them. It's important to understand that out of bad things *come* good. Your child grows through every experience, and your child MUST be involved in his own solutions.

To illustrate this point, an excerpt from *THIS IS OUT OF CONTROL! A Practical Guide to Managing Life's Conflicts* is provided.

> There seems to be an instant human reaction to jump to quick conclusions about whether a situation is a blessing or a curse. The reality is that we may not know for quite some time if what has happened is negative or positive. Often, what initially seems to be a blessing has some negative consequences. What initially seems to be a tragedy or a trial will result in some positive consequences.
>
> There are situations in which you may not ever know if there were positives. When I am running late for unforeseen reasons, I try to remember that there may be some unknown reason that I am late. This train of thought always makes me think of an experience that my family and I had while on vacation. My family and I were visiting a friend. We were to leave to attend a wedding on that Saturday, and would be staying overnight. With several of us

to get ready and packed, we were fairly rushed. We probably could have planned better. In fact, I'm sure we could have planned better! There was much hurrying and double-checking. Finally we were ready to go. Everyone was organized, clean and looked great. We had a bit of time to spare and could have a fairly leisurely trip to the wedding, a trip that should take one and a half hours. We'd have a little time to visit before the wedding. Okay, let's go, hurry up. Ummm... but where are the keys?

We searched, everyone in the house searched. Very calmly I might add. We decided to believe that we were meant to slow down for some reason. We turned the house upside down. We unpacked the luggage we were leaving behind and packed it again. We unpacked the luggage we were taking along and packed it again. We realized that one set of keys were in the locked vehicle, but there was still no sign of the other set. Forty-five minutes later, after we'd called to let them know we'd be late, and as I was calling a locksmith, the keys were found under the corner of a mat. That area had been searched several times previously. We made it to the wedding just minutes before it started.

Were we fortunate, or unfortunate? Would something tragic have happened if we had kept on rushing? We'll never know. What we do know is that taking it easy, and not deciding something is terrible right of the bat, keeps emotions more balanced. Problem solving skills are enhanced, rather than being impaired by anger or other high emotion. Learning experiences are more easily identified when emotions are balanced. Coming into a wedding late isn't the end of your world, getting into a traffic accident on the way there may be.

It can also be explained like this:

You don't always know if you are lucky or unlucky as soon as something happens. The things that seem unlucky sometimes turn out to be really good. The things that seem lucky sometimes turn out to be really bad.

When something unlucky happens, it is important to wait a little bit in order to see if the results are good or bad.

Sometimes, instead of waiting, we get upset right away. Not now, but RIGHT NOW! This can end up making things worse. If you get a poor mark on a test and you immediately react in a negative way, you might not handle telling your parents very well. You might be so upset that you get angry with them and say something that you don't mean or that gets you into trouble. If you take the time to think about how you want to react instead of just getting angry, you will probably be able to resolve the problem in a more positive way. You will also be less likely to use bully actions if you think about how you want to react. You will also be able to handle bully actions against you better.

Activities:

Write the words "Lucky or unlucky" on a piece of paper and put it somewhere it can be seen. Go back to this idea when something bad happens.

Have your child teach this idea to another adult.

With your child, brainstorm some examples of where something seemed bad and turned out good or seemed good and turned out bad.

If she is unable to come up with examples, here are some ideas:

Has your bicycle ever broken down, but it was close to your house and you could just walk home? And then your dad helped you fix it and you had a really good time together?

Have you ever received a present that you thought you didn't want and then it turned out that you liked it or it was useful?

Protection Twenty Four: Control

We spend a lot of time fighting against, and being anxious or angry about things we don't control! This lesson is intended to remind you and your child, that there are things we can control, and things we can't.

The following excerpt is taken from *THIS IS OUT OF CONTROL! A Practical Guide to Managing Life's Conflicts*:

> We spend a lot of time fretting about people and situations over which we have no control. We don't control our friends, families or spouses. Control of our children is lost before they leave the womb.
>
> We can't influence others by trying to make them be or become someone who acts the way we want them to. The only thing we have control over is ourselves, and the only way we can influence the behavior of others is through our own behavior. When we change our reactions, it often causes a chain reaction that changes the way others relate to us.
>
> An action plan is a plan for change. Rather than spending a lot of time on an action plan that tries to control others, know what you control.
>
> Listing the things that concern you helps you to evaluate which of them you can control. Use the list to determine what you directly influence - your own behavior, your attitude, your ability to work hard towards achievements. Any items you can change yourself, are the items over which you have total control. There are other people and circumstances that you can influence with your own behavior, but

over which you don't have total control. This might include family members, friends, co-workers or situations at work. Place your focus on the areas that you directly control.

I control my actions.
I can hit or not hit.
I can yell or not yell.
I can smoke or not smoke.
I can drink alcohol or not drink alcohol.

I control my thoughts.
I can look at the positive or the negative side of things.
I can work to have balanced thinking.
I can know that my automatic thoughts are not true.

I control my behaviors.
I can be kind or mean.
I can be respectful or disrespectful.
I can be helpful or unhelpful.

I have no control over...
other people.
the weather.
where or how my parents live.
what my friends or siblings do.
other people's schedules.
other people's thoughts.

Activities:

Use the list above to talk about which things your child has control of, and which they do not control. Discuss how they have control, what actions they could take and what impact their actions might have on different situations. Make a list with your child.

Go to http://nosuchthingasabully.com to play some fun games and answer some questions about what they control about the game.

Plans to Review

Develop a plan for using this material into the future. Keep this book at hand, and review it periodically. The most effective way to incorporate these ideas into your life, and your child's life is to use them daily. Remember that keeping the lines of communication open with your child and teaching your child to be a strong communicator is going to make your child resistant to using bully actions or victim responses. Not only are you making your child resistant to these actions, you are also providing the strong communication and thinking skills that your child will need in order to maintain positive relationships throughout his life.

References

Canadian Public Health Association, *Assessment Toolkit for Bullying, Harassment, and Peer Relations at school,* http://bit.ly/4DOCns

Coloroso, Barbara. The Bully, The Bullied and the Bystander. (2004)

Dana. Dr. Daniel, Conflict Resolution: Mediation Tools for Everyday Worklife. (2001)

deBecker, Gavin. Protecting the Gift: Keeping Children and Teenagers Safe (And Parents Sane). (1999)

Goleman, Daniel. Emotional Intelligence: Why it Can Matter More Than IQ. (1996)

Rigby, Ken. University of Australia. Definition adapted from Ken Rigby, and used by permission, www.kenrigby.net

Dawn-Marie Wesley's Story

http://www.cbc.ca/news/story/2002/03/25/wesley020325.html

http://www.cbc.ca/news/story/2002/05/15/sentence_circle020515.html

http://ratsandbullies.com/

http://www2.canada.com/windsorstar/news/story.html?id=e5c4e564-111b-4782-b56d-05e01a42defe&k=51521

Emmet Fralick's Story

http://ctv.ca/servlet/ArticleNews/story/CTVNews/20020723/halifax_bully_020722?s_name=&no_ads=

http://stopbullying.ns.ca/pages/stories.html

http://cbc.ca/canada/story/2003/01/02/bully030102.html

Contacts for *No Such Thing as a Bully*®

Email:
ron@nosuchthingasabully.com
kelly@nosuchthingasabully.com

Twitter:
http://twitter.com/4nstaab

Facebook:
http://facebook.com/nosuchthingasabully
http://facebook.com/bully.stakeout

Phone:
587-333-8107